Horatio and Fortinbras: Abridged Edition

By Bluebell Dewpetal

Copyright page:

While every precaution has been taken in the preparation of the book, the publisher assumes no responsibility for errors or omissions, or for damages resulting from the use of the information contained herein.

HORATIO AND FORTINBRAS: ABRIDGED EDITION

Written by Bluebell Dewpetal

Cover illustration by Bluebell Dewpetal

Published by Bluebell Dewpetal, 2025

Copyright © 2025 Bluebell Dewpetal

All rights reserved.

ISBN EBOOK: 978-1-7645266-1-6

ISBN PAPERBACK: 978-1-7645266-3-0

All characters and events depicted in this play are fictitious. Any resemblance to real persons outside the early modern period, living or dead, is purely coincidental.

Contents

Title page 1
Copyright page: 2
Contents 3
Preface: 7
Characters: 9
Act 1: 11
   Scene 1: *Grave* 11
   Scene 2: *Outside the Elsinore castle* 12
   Scene 3: *Inside Fortinbras's room* 14
   Scene 4: *Outside, in Elsinore's castle grounds* 17
   Scene 5: *At a stable of Elsinore Castle* 19
   Scene 6: *At the front of Elsinore castle's gate* 22
   Scene 7: *Inside Elsinore castle, a room with a map.* ... 26
   Scene 8: *Afternoon, in the castle* 32
   Scene 9: *In that middle section of Elsinore's castle/Kronborg castle* 33
   Scene 10: *In Elsinore Town* 34
   Scene 11: *Fortinbras's quarters* 38
   Scene 12: *Elsinore Gardens* 42
   Scene 13: *Akershus Fortress* 43
   Scene 14: *At the Swedish Castle* 47
   Scene 15: *At a large room in Elsinore castle* 48
   Scene 16: *Grave* 49
   Scene 17: *Elsinore shores* 53
   Scene 18: *At the Elsinore castle stables* 54

Scene 19: *Somewhere inside Elsinore castle* 56
Scene 20: *Elsinore castle casemates* 58
Scene 21: *Outside of Elsinore castle* 61
Scene 22: *At Elsinore town* 64
Scene 23: *Fortinbras's quarters* 67
Scene 24: *Shores of Poland* 73
Scene 25: *Helsingborg* 74
Scene 26: *Scania, Denmark* 76
Scene 27: *Close to Stockholm* 78
Scene 28: *Tre Kronor Castle* 80
Scene 29: *Ship* 85
Scene 30: *Somewhere in Elsinore Castle* 89
Scene 31: *Middle floors of the castle* 90
Scene 32: *Another floor of Elsinore Castle* 94
Scene 34: *Elsinore Town* 97
Scene 35: *An empty field at the edge of Denmark* 100
Act 2: 103
Scene 36: *Outside of Elsinore castle* 107
Scene 37: *North Sea, on a boat* 113
Scene 38: *Oslo Castle / Akershus Fortress* 118
Scene 39: *Outside in Oslo, next to the sea* 123
Scene 40: *Castle cells* 127
Scene 41: *Ship on the North Sea* 134
Scene 42: *Skagan Shores* 138
Scene 43: *Skagen* 144
Scene 44: *Skagen Shores* 149
Scene 45: *Outside the Oslo castle* 151

Scene 46: *Inside the Oslo Castle* 155
Scene 47: *Water's edge in Oslo* 157
Scene 48: *A Church* 162
Scene 49: *Captain's house, outside* 163
Scene 50: *North sea, on a boat* 164
Scene 51: *Outside Elsinore Castle* 172
Scene 52: *Grave with the bush* 176
Scene 53: *Elsinore town* 184
Scene 54: *Graveyard* 189
Scene 55: *Water's Edge at Oslo* 192
Scene 56: *Lonely water's edge, somewhere in Norway* 193
End notes 202

Preface:

Hi. This was my attempt at a *Hamlet* sequel I wrote when I was younger.

For this release, it's the abridged version of the story that was around 36,000 words. This shortened version is around 28,500 words long. It's still long and would have a long runtime if ever performed, but hopefully the pacing is more even.

If you're new to *Hamlet*, I tried to leave enough context for newcomers to understand, but you might want see *Hamlet* for yourself.

I've been debating keeping this story released or not. I'm not saying this story is haunted or cursed, however, my life had been going through a long rough patch after I had written it. Call it superstition, I think this story wants to be released, whether I like it or not.

About the author:

I won't reuse an alias connected to this story for future stories.

I do not have social media connected to this story.

Any contact details you find related to this story could be or is outdated.

Characters:

Some of the characters:

Fortinbras: Prince of Norway, now king of Denmark.

Horatio: Hamlet's friend, now reluctantly Fortinbras's advisor.

Fortinjambes: Fortinbras's younger sister. Norwegian princess.

Marcellus: Sentinel at Elsinore, Denmark.

Captain: Fortinbras's army captain

Stable-hand: Looks after the horses. Close to Fortinbras. Sometimes referred to as Aksel.

Prince Norway: Norwegian Prince. Fortinbras's cousin, son of Norway's current king. Sometimes referred to as Justin.

Fortincoeur: Placeholder name. Fortinbras's mother.

Swedish King

Polish Prince

The other characters could be either recurring characters from *Hamlet*, or they'll just be listed by their role (e.g. Peasant, pirate) when they appear.

You might see placeholder names throughout.

Act 1:

Scene 1: *Grave*

At Prince Hamlet's grave, at night. Enter Horatio, then the Gravedigger

GRAVEDIGGER

    Here for your nightly nap upon the prince's grave?

HORATIO

    I do no such thing. Besides, why are you here, instead of doing your work?

GRAVEDIGGER

    I was once told that there was a phantom that haunts here every night, lengthily recounting stories from the King's castle in the day.

HORATIO

    A phantom!? I beg of you, tell me more!

GRAVEDIGGER

    He's about this tall, and this high.

HORATIO

    You're describing me, aren't you?

GRAVEDIGGER

    Couldn't help but notice you have the habits of a phantom.

HORATIO

    Go back to your business, and begone!

Exit Gravedigger.

Horatio sits down and talks to Hamlet's grave.

HORATIO

    The gravedigger is right. What is there to say? You've been hearing the same misery from me about being without you these past six months. I still haven't returned to studying at Wittenberg. I still fill my time with servant work at the castle or whatever else Fortinbras has planned for that day, and everybody else has already moved on now that Fortinbras is Denmark's king. Maybe it's time I stopped bothering you with my inability, and make a step to do the same…

Exit Horatio

Scene 2: *Outside the Elsinore castle*

Outside the Elsinore castle, still night.

Enter Horatio, Marcellus the Sentinel

MARCELLUS

    Halt! Who is there?

HORATIO

    Just Horatio.

MARCELLUS

    Ah, Horatio, hello. It would be preferable that you do your exercise at a more reasonable hour. Even though I know your nightly schedule, your shadowed figure in the dark still alerts me every night.

HORATIO

    My mind is too restless these nights…

MARCELLUS

    Your restlessness is matched by our king. Earlier, he told me to tell you, that he needed your advice for something, and to come to his quarters, though I have no detail on what.

HORATIO

    How remarkable. Thank you for telling me. I'll be away now, and I hope your watch will be uneventful.

MARCELLUS

    Good-bye Horatio.

Exit Horatio, Marcellus.

Scene 3: *Inside Fortinbras's room*

Inside Fortinbras's room in the castle.

Enter Fortinbras. He is seated at a desk with papers.

Enter Horatio.

Horatio knocks on the door.

HORATIO

    You have finally have a use for me?

Fortinbras unlocks the door.

FORTINBRAS

    You talk as if your position as advisor is a joke. Indeed I do. Take one of those chairs and sit down here.

Horatio takes a chair and sits down at Fortinbras's desk

FORTINBRAS

    These papers. One is a letter from my uncle, who likes to question too much about my life because the king of Norway has nothing better to do. I'd like you to write back to him for me.

And the other is for my darling mother and sister. They're not replying to my letters. At all. Horatio, do you think I'm boring?

HORATIO

    I can't say I particularly care for your ninetieth discussion about boats and horses.

FORTINBRAS

    Exactly. I am entirely ordinary and so particularly uninteresting.

Dear lovely mother and little sister, I've brought my current and temporary advisor Horatio to delight you in this letter. He is a scholar who had studied in Wittenberg. Written below is his mind at work.

Fortinbras hands the letter over to Horatio. Horatio tries to start, but cannot.

FORTINBRAS

    They may be Norwegian royalty, but even if you write vulgar things, they won't mind.

Horatio still cannot write anything.

FORTINBRAS

    A scholar inexperienced at writing? What, have you never written to your family before? Had Hamlet let you use a messenger?

HORATIO

    My family? I haven't.

FORTINBRAS

    You may be a man, but I find my love for my family has not died with age. What rift is between you?

HORATIO

    You pry as much as your uncle. My mother and father were dead, before I went away far enough to write letters.

FORTINBRAS

How unfortunate. Have you avenged them?

HORATIO

I cannot avenge against madness, grief, or their own hands. I ran from my hometown and never dared to venture back.

FORTINBRAS

An excruciating position, to have no villain to fight against, with the hopes that defeat may ease your emotional turmoil. Write whatever comes to mind, since you say your mind so well. That is how I write to my family.

HORATIO

[saying aloud while writing] You may have heard tales of Hamlet, the Mad Prince of Denmark, but he only acted in that manner during the final times of his life. As I knew him, he was a most dear friend. He had endless wit and jokes and…

Horatio starts crying.

FORTINBRAS

Wipe your tears. If you cry all over your writing, no one will be able to read the ink.

Take these papers so you can continue working on them. You are dismissed.

Exit Horatio.

FORTINBRAS

      Funny man. So stuck within his head, he takes little note he's writing about the son of the man who killed my mother's husband.

Sweet and noble and loving Hamlet, the sun had shone brightly on Denmark's jewel. He was only a prince, but his death has not stopped his sparkling light beaming into the memories of the Danes.

For most of his life, this prince had joyously lived on my former home. Laughing, studying, and being loved by his people. A clear mind in the graces of God. If Denmark's lands had stayed shared between our fathers, so would our joys.

Yet his father turned mine into sliced food for maggots! Old Fortinbras's lands, life, and family's future on these lands, ousted in a whim. In replacement, I received a life entrenched in vengeance for my father's honour…

How do these dead men still stir me so much? The past has passed. Denmark's entirety in my possession. I am home again. All there is left to do, is to seize Denmark's joys!

Exit Fortinbras

Scene 4: *Outside, in Elsinore's castle grounds*

Daytime. Outside, in Elsinore's castle grounds.

Enter Fortinbras, and Horatio.

HORATIO

    Why am I here? Haven't I already been tasked with writing letters?

FORTINBRAS

    You have, but I imagine you'll need fresh air, after spending so long writing a letter to my uncle. What do you think about having a short fencing match with those men over there? Or me?

HORATIO

    I cannot bear to look at anything fencing-related. Must you torture me with the reminders of what happened to Hamlet and Laertes?

FORTINBRAS

    Pause

    Some players will be at the castle today, performing a comedy. I'm not particularly interested in today's play, but will watching them delight you?

HORATIO

    No. Sometimes comedy has some sort of misfortune at its core. A man falls down, and people laugh at his pain.

FORTINBRAS

    How about wine? It makes most men somewhat joyful.

HORATIO

    No. Claudius's rule has… given us Danes a reputation for being drunkards.

FORTINBRAS

    There's a wonderful brook nearby that shall satisfy your fondness for water. It reminds me of Norway's fjords, though it vastly lacks in size in comparison.

HORATIO

    Any more of your merry suggestions, and my mind shall become merrier than is reasonable!

FORTINBRAS

    [aside] So those horrid events still weigh on his mind…

    I'd rather that you stay, reasonable Horatio, but I have one last suggestion, actually, a command.

Pause

I know someone most delightful. Follow me.

Exit Fortinbras, Horatio exits slowly and reluctantly.

Scene 5: *At a stable of Elsinore Castle*

At a stable of Elsinore castle.

Enter (peg-legged) Stable-Hand, Fortinbras, Horatio

FORTINBRAS

    How now, my brilliant stable-hand?

STABLE-HAND

> Merrily trudging around as always. Greetings, Horatio!

HORATIO

> Your majesty, is this the person you spoke of?

FORTINBRAS

> He is not, but he is a delightful person anyway.

STABLE-HAND

> And I would say the same to you!

(to Horatio)

Do you want to know how I got this leg?

HORATIO

> Not particularly.

STABLE-HAND

> I'll tell you anyway!

When Fortinbras and I were children, one game we played was seeing who could pull the most horse tails. Unfortunately, I lost one time.

FORTINBRAS

> And now he is handsomely compensated by being employed forever, by me.

STABLE-HAND

> So I am a victor in one sense!

HORATIO

>Wonderful…

STABLE-HAND

>But not as wonderful as this beauty! Hear it all from Fortinbras!

FORTINBRAS

>Here is Mourner! Isn't she lovely? I've known her ever since she was born! She is my own daughter. Denmark is the greatest gift for her, or perhaps it is the other way around.

Enter black horse prop

HORATIO

>She is certainly a horse.

FORTINBRAS

>A horse that wears the midnight sky, both in darkness and light. Appreciate the spectacle of how her coat shines with its own stars under the sun!

HORATIO

>Charming… Why is she called Mourner?

FORTINBRAS

>She mourns for dead men on the battlefield! It's very hard to have funerals for shredded bits of bodies, their families can't attend. But at least they have a wonderful maiden like her mourning for them!

Chattering in the distance

Do you hear that noise?

STABLE-HAND

It sounds like a whole party of people.

FORTINBRAS

But not loud enough to be an army. I'll bring Mourner with me and see who has arrived.

Exit Fortinbras

STABLE-HAND

Have you ever ridden a horse?

HORATIO

A few times. I will be fine on foot, and go to it slowly, in case this sudden arrival has malicious intent.

Exit Stable-Hand, Horatio

Scene 6: *At the front of Elsinore castle's gate*

At the front of Elsinore castle's gate.

Enter Marcellus

Enter Fortinjambes and the rest of her party

Enter Fortinbras

MARCELLUS

She claims to be the princess of Norway?

FORTINBRAS

It is too bad that Denmark was acquired in the strangest way…But it's better than never having it! Are you finally here to claim Denmark's lands for yourself as well?

FORTINJAMBES

Actually, we received your letter detailing how horribly sick you were, and to bring Norway's best doctors and nurses, and that I should come along too, with the greatest haste. But as I can see, you have made a most splendid recovery to be riding with Mourner right now!

FORTINBRAS

Consider me perplexed, because I have recovered from nothing. I've never sent such a letter asking for all this help, for this strange illness I've never had…

FORTINJAMBES

Then what is this?

Fortinjambes hands over a letter and envelope to Fortinbras

FORTINBRAS

Have I an identical stranger as well somewhere, that could make such an excellent forgery? If he were not the cause of such a strange situation, I would follow your example and befriend him.

Enter Horatio

FORTINBRAS

    This is Horatio, my advisor. Horatio, look, what do you think of this forgery?

HORATIO

    It does look like your handwriting, from what I've seen of it. And a perfect copy of the Danish seal.

Horatio hands the letter back to Fortinbras

FORTINBRAS

    It would be rude of me to keep all my guests outside. Dismount your horses and come into the castle. We have a group of players performing a comedy, so you can relax after your weary travels. We will discuss this strange occurrence tomorrow.

Exit Fortinbras, Fortinjambes and her party

MARCELLUS

    Do my eyes deceive me, or has seeing this maiden brought back some liveliness to you?

HORATIO

    It's less to do with Fortinbras's sister or any sort of joy in life, and more to do with my newfound goal outliving Fortinbras, so I wouldn't have one of his horses attend my funeral.

MARCELLUS

    What strange words! Horatio, are you alright?

HORATIO

There's nothing mad within me. Fortinbras is the bold one.

MARCELLUS

Ah yes, I do remark that his horse is black, though I didn't think the king would do such a thing. I apologise for any insult.

HORATIO

I know you meant no harm.

MARCELLUS

I'm going to watch the comedy, and someone will take my place. Are you coming?

HORATIO

I think I will stay outside for some more time. Good-bye Marcellus.

MARCELLUS

Good-bye Horatio!

Exit Marcellus

HORATIO

For a moment, Marcellus thought I could possibly be a madman, and yesternight the gravedigger mocked me. Do I look so disorderly? I must steel myself up. Nothing bodes well for anybody thought of as a madman…

Exit Horatio

Scene 7: *Inside Elsinore castle, a room with a map.*

Inside Elsinore castle, a room with a map.

Enter Fortinbras, Horatio, Fortinjambes, Captain, the Stable-Hand, Voltimand and Cornelius who are ambassadors of Denmark, and whatever other people are important when the king makes decisions.

They all sit around a table. Half of the people look barely awake.

COURTIER 1

     Unless I was mistaken, wasn't this issue supposed to be discussed tomorrow?

FORTINBRAS

     It is past midnight. Tomorrow is today.

COURTIER 2

     It is still dark, and I can't imagine many of us can give good advice when our eyes are drawn to sleep.

FORTINBRAS

     Just use your hands to hold your eyes open. Easy.

Now, the present problem is finding out who has forged the letter, and to what purpose. Fortinjambes. Tell me what you know about how you received that letter.

FORTINJAMBES

> Two people who claimed to be ambassadors from Denmark gave it to us.

I simply assumed your usual ambassadors were on some other business, and with the letter looking so much like yours, we never questioned it.

FORTINBRAS

> So did you and mother receive my four letters from my usual ambassadors?

FORTINJAMBES

> Yes.

FORTINBRAS

> But you've never replied? Not even to news about me becoming king?

FORTINJAMBES

> I can't deny it.

FORTINBRAS

> Why?

FORTINJAMBES

> The dog eats all the letters.

FORTINBRAS

> Really? All four of them?

FORTINJAMBES

> Really.

FORTINBRAS

Those two impersonators, what do you suspect they could be?

FORTINJAMBES

They did their best Danish impressions, because I was unable to tell otherwise. But there is the possibility that they could be thieves and pirates.

HORATIO

I have heard about pirates on the North Sea, between Denmark and England. If some pirates have migrated to between Denmark and Norway, or if new pirates have shown up, they could be quite troublesome.

CAPTAIN

Can someone explain how these thieves and sea-thieves would have somehow managed to not only impersonate ambassadors, but also Fortinbras's immaculate handwriting, and the Danish Seal?

FORTINJAMBES

Pirates can be quite talented. Perhaps one had snuck into the castle at Oslo and forged the letters and seal.

FORTINBRAS

Goodness gracious, pirates sneaking into Akershus Fortress, to steal and forge letters? How can Norway be having such incompetent security when their king is already bedridden!?

FORTINJAMBES

    Do not worry, our Uncle has known about these pirates for a while, and your cousin is eliminating them this very second. Leave Norway alone for a while, and they will send a letter when every pirate has sunken.

FORTINBRAS

    Leave it alone? You could have gotten kidnapped.

That's it, I'm expanding Denmark's Navy.

HORATIO

    But Claudius had already built plenty of ships while he ruled, in anticipation of you invading Denmark. It will cost even more money.

FORTINBRAS

    Clearly it's not enough if we're still having these sorts of pirate problems. I would like to eliminate the pirates myself as soon as possible, and together with Norway's fleet, we shall have complete control of the North Sea and Baltic Sea.

With control of the seas and for the service of ridding the pirates, we have reason to increase the tolls at the Sound Strait. It will do well for Denmark's wealth, and allow continued operations for our navy.

FORTINJAMBES

    Must you really battle against these pirates when our Uncle and cousin is already handling them?

FORTINBRAS

    They're handling it terribly. If Justin does not wish for me to fight, then nothing will be in his favour, and Norway's army will have to fight these pirates alongside mine anyway.

HORATIO

    Who's Justin?

FORTINJAMBES

    Prince Justin. Our older cousin in Norway, son of the current king.

FORTINBRAS

    Fortinjambes, I know the letter was a forgery, but please don't venture back to Norway while pirates infest our surroundings. My, no, our kingdom, is perfectly liveable.

Voltimand, Cornelius, you will go through Sweden to give a message to my family about my participation in the battle against pirates. Tomorrow I will meet with you about the message you will send.

I thank everyone for your input. Now you are dismissed.

Exit everyone except Fortinbras, Stable-hand

STABLE-HAND

    That was amusing. You seem so eager to fight these pirates.

FORTINBRAS

    I am. It will be the most exciting thing I've done as king. As much as I love traversing Denmark's flat lands, a part of me has become restless, and my sailing skills will atrophy without use.

STABLE-HAND

    Ah, another good-bye. Since this is a purely naval battle, while you are away, who will give Mourner her exercise?

FORTINBRAS

    Do you know if Horatio is able? I've seen the enlightening effect seeing Mourner up close has had on him. I think he was more intrigued by Mourner than this meeting, or anything else I've done while ruling Denmark after Hamlet's funeral. If he isn't, we can train him to ride horses, so when I leave, he can truly meet Mourner.

STABLE-HAND

    Horatio says he has ridden a horse a few times, so he would do well with more training. Perhaps by the time you return from sea, Mourner will have absorbed his gloominess, leaving him unrecognisable to my eyes!

FORTINBRAS

    And if it's not Mourner's presence, then perhaps Denmark's wealth after the battles shall impress the melancholiest Dane I've ever seen. Should that day come where Horatio is unrecognisable, I will provide you with a new description for you to recognise him by!

I'll be gone now. Goodnight Aksel.

STABLE-HAND

>Goodnight Fortinbras.

Exit Fortinbras, Stable-hand

Scene 8: *Afternoon, in the castle*

Afternoon, in the castle

Enter Fortinbras, Doctor 1, Doctor 2

Enter Horatio, hidden at the edge of the stage, tailing the doctors

FORTINBRAS

>*[aside]* These tailing doctors! Have they nothing better to do?

DOCTOR 1

>Your majesty, how are you?

FORTINBRAS

>As fine as ever. I was not ill yesterday, and I am not ill today. If I were, I would not be meeting with my captain later today to plan the building of the navy.

I see that having come all the way here, but finding that your intended task is nothing but a forged fantasy is causing aimless wandering. I shall give you all an aim. You doctors, Fortinjambes and the rest of the arrival party, will go to Elsinore Town to amuse yourselves. I will ask Horatio to guide you once I find him. You will all meet at the centre courtyard of the castle, where the fountain is.

Exit Fortinbras, doctors, Horatio

Scene 9: *In that middle section of Elsinore's castle/Kronborg castle*

In that middle section of Elsinore's castle/Kronborg castle

Enter doctors, Fortinjambes, other people in the party

Enter Horatio (but he's hiding behind a fountain prop)

FORTINJAMBES

    Is Horatio here? He asked me to meet the rest of the group here.

DOCTOR 1

    I've yet to spot him.

FORTINJAMBES

    How is Fortinbras?

DOCTOR 2

    Restless. He moves as if stopping once will stop him forever. He walks day and night.

FORTINJAMBES

    That behaviour does not indicate much, he's always been like that. Has he voiced any suspicions?

DOCTOR 2

    No, but he was bothered by us observing him, and ordered us to amuse ourselves at town.

FORTINJAMBES

    So we shall.

Pause

Horatio finally reveals himself

FORTINJAMBES

    Ah Horatio, you have arrived! We came to this castle so speedily, that we didn't appreciate town!

HORATIO

    Are you all fine walking to town on foot? I'm not particularly experienced with riding horses.

FORTINJAMBES

    We will be fine.

Exit Horatio, Fortinjambes, doctors, the rest of Fortinjambe's arrival party

Scene 10: *In Elsinore Town*

In Elsinore Town

Enter Horatio, Fortinjambes, doctors, rest of the arrival party, and townspeople.

TOWNSPERSON

    Horatio? With a noblewoman like that? Impossible!

TOWNSPERSON 2

    I can't ever believe a woman would ever be interested in a man that's all Hamlet, Hamlet, Hamlet. It's all I ever hear from him.

HORATIO

    She's a new arrival to Denmark from Norway. Fortinbras asked me to show her around the town.

TOWNSPERSON

    Yes of course it was orders from the king, no woman would ever want to come close to you otherwise.

TOWNSPERSON 2

    She does look like His Majesty. Do you happen to be his sister, the princess, he talks about?

FORTINJAMBES

    Perhaps.

TOWNSPERSON 2

    How wonderful! Then please, tell your brother this. Our existing navy is big enough to fight a few pirates! Even the Norwegians from Fortinbras's army that live here now are complaining.

TOWNPERSON

    Exactly! Our life was perfectly relaxed, until this morning's notice.

Fortinbras's Norwegian army-men that live here say that thousands of them went all the way to Poland, all to risk their lives for a useless scrap of land his father lost decades ago, before coming here. Six months on the throne, this almost-stranger earned merely by walking into Denmark's tragedy at the right time, and already he has the gall to command us into a battle we don't need! Norwegians, Danes, does he have value for life?

HORATIO

    Thank you for your thoughts.

FORTINJAMBES

    The decision to expand the navy doesn't seem popular.

Exit Townsperson

NURSE 1

    I would like to try my luck with a townsperson.

Enter a young townsperson walking by

NURSE 1

    Hello, I am a visitor from Norway. May I ask if you know anything strange about your king?

YOUNG TOWNSPERSON

    No, but I can tell you something strange about the previous royalty! Claudius secretly killed King Hamlet with poison, and then Prince Hamlet found out, and went so mad, he took a sword, then sliced up everyone important in the castle, and then himself! We call him

Mad Hamlet the Slayer!

HORATIO

[aside] How is it that the truths about Hamlet slowly disappear day by day!? Despite our best efforts, did the word of how clever and noble Hamlet was, fail to spread? Or was it transformed into this flightful fantasy that thrills the minds of children? Oh, I must try not to weep. I lived to tell Hamlet's story, and my life has amounted to this.

NURSE 1

Thank you, child. I found your story quite interesting.

Young Townsperson skips off

FORTINJAMBES

Is this true?

HORATIO

No!

Sorry, your highness, I meant not at all. Hamlet was not like that, mostly.

FORTINJAMBES

Mostly?

HORATIO

He did stab someone, who was intruding in his mother's bedroom. What truly happened was that Claudius had poisoned King Hamlet while he was sleeping in a garden. Then Queen Gertrude, Laertes and Prince Hamlet were poisoned by the wine and weapons during a fencing duel. Prince Hamlet eliminated Claudius before the poison had felled him. Then your brother returned from a victory in Poland, walked into the castle, and received the crown by Prince Hamlet's dying words.

FORTINJAMBES

      Huh. I thought the time he'd finally get Denmark for himself would be a lot more impressive than walking in at an odd time.

HORATIO

      Ummm… where next? How about Saint Olaf's church now? It's just over there.

FORTINJAMBES

      I see this land in the distance, that is quite unlike Norway's. Take me to the edge of town first, so I can look at it better.

HORATIO

      Let's go.

Exit Horatio, Fortinjambes, doctors, townspeople

Scene 11: *Fortinbras's quarters*

Night

Fortinbras's quarters

Enter Fortinbras, Fortinjambes, Horatio. Fortinbras is at his desk.

FORTINBRAS

    How was the town? How was Denmark?

FORTINJAMBES

    It's fine. It's flat. Very flat compared to Norway.

FORTINBRAS

    [aside] Is that all?

You'll learn to appreciate it. To me, Denmark is just as beautiful as it was in my childhood memories, and I'm glad it's finally all mine. Or ours.

FORTINJAMBES

    Maybe you just happen to like it more because you were born here. Why not make this island of Denmark's, or all of Denmark, part of Norway again? It'd be easier for the family to work together.

FORTINBRAS

    And go back to being just a prince of Norway when I can be king of Denmark? Not a chance! I like this independence.

Pause

Horatio, what is that look on your face? It appears something is troubling you, but you are holding back. Let no fear of punishment stop the truth.

HORATIO

    The Danish townspeople have little pride in you. They don't want to give up their lives for a former Norwegian Prince who has been king for six months that they hardly know, they don't want to battle with the pirates, and they think our Navy is big enough. I really would reconsider fighting against the pirates.

FORTINBRAS

Is that so? The townspeople speak too early. Fortinjambes almost got kidnapped and I'd rather not wait until merchants do complain about pirates interrupting their contact to other countries. I'm planning to tour Denmark again and convince us all that there's no gamble in this because we will have the most impressive navy. We can't lose. Once the battles are won, prosperity will come to Denmark. They will be glad for that.

Fortinjambes yawns.

FORTINJAMBES

I'm tired, I'm going to bed now. Good-bye you two.

Exit Fortinjambes

FORTINBRAS

She left at a good time, because now I can tell you to stop having your wandering eyes wander onto my sister! She has no interest in men like you! If your eyes must drift in search of her, then let them drift onto my face. We have enough resemblance to each other, and it is good for subjects to admire your king.

HORATIO

I have no such thoughts about your sister! Only that she and her party are suspicious figures.

FORTINBRAS

    She flits about as she pleases because my mother and I spoiled her too much! Every night as children, Fortinjambes and I would act out plans about how we'd exact revenge against King Hamlet and get our land back. She always wanted to be a spy amongst the Danes.

HORATIO

    I have no qualms against her spirit. It is that earlier today, I saw the doctors saying to her that you had no suspicions about something, and that you were bothered by their observations. They didn't explain what suspicions they're hoping that you don't have, but something is amiss…

FORTINBRAS

    I will talk to her. Thank you, Horatio. By the way, go to the stables tomorrow at noon.

HORATIO

    What for?

FORTINBRAS

    I've decided you should learn how to ride a horse.

HORATIO

    If you wish…

Fortinbras, may I ask you a question?

FORTINBRAS

    You already have, but you may ask another one.

HORATIO

>The town tells strange tales about Hamlet. Are any of these tales from your own doing?

FORTINBRAS

>I've only ever told Denmark exactly what you have told me. I may have envied Prince Hamlet, but besmirching his memory would be ungrateful to someone whose final words were kindness to me.

HORATIO

>Thank you…

[aside] If not from him, then why do these tales that undo my work exist?

Exit Horatio, Fortinbras

Scene 12: *Elsinore Gardens*

Elsinore Gardens

Enter Fortinbras, Fortinjambes

FORTINBRAS

>Hello sister. Yesterday Horatio said that you and your doctors were talking about the possibility that I suspect something, and looking for rumours about me. Can you explain yourselves?

FORTINJAMBES

    That Horatio! While I'm here, I thought I might as well surprise you with a gift you would like, and I had the doctors attempt to observe you. I had not seen you in a while and perhaps your tastes had changed. Some of the doctors are also too attached to that forgery letter, and still insist on searching for this non-existent illness! If the doctors bother you too much, I can call them off.

FORTINBRAS

    How thoughtful of my dear sister! Alright then, you can go, but please, call off the doctors.

FORTINJAMBES

    I will.

Exit Fortinjambes

FORTINBRAS

    Despite her reassurance, I feel unsettled, and I wish I did not. It is probably nothing. I need to be capable now. After all, Justin always told me that feelings with no reason from which they stem should be pushed aside.

Exit Fortinbras

Scene 13: *Akershus Fortress*

At the Norwegian, Oslo Castle, Akershus Fortress

Enter Fortincoeur, Voltimand, Cornelius

VOLTIMAND

We have a message from your son. He says he will participate in the battle against the pirates between Denmark and Norway, in around six months' time when all the new ships that Denmark is building are finished.

FORTINCOEUR

Wasn't his cousin's army going to handle the pirates?

VOLTIMAND

Fortinbras is not ill, the letter was a forgery. He is fit to battle against the pirates. He wants you to increase the security for the castle, because he finds it disappointing that a forgery letter can possibly originate from a thief stealing his letters in the castle, and put his sister in danger.

CORNELIUS

Fortinbras also absolutely refused to back away from the battle against the pirates, and Norway will have to fight alongside Denmark. Fortinbras hopes Denmark's naval forces will control the North and Baltic Seas after ridding the pirates.

FORTINCOEUR

Is that all?

CORNELIUS

Yes. Is there anything you would like to say in reply to him?

FORTINCOEUR

> Is it impossible to convince him not to fight the pirates?

VOLTIMAND

> Before we left, he anticipated this question. He says it's impossible. No bribery will stop him.

FORTINCOEUR

> Then I have nothing else. Take a rest somewhere in our castle before you leave tomorrow.

VOLTIMAND, CORNELIUS

> Thank you.

Exit Voltimand, Cornelius

FORTINCOEUR

> There has been a grave miscalculation. Prince Justin!

Enter Prince Norway

PRINCE NORWAY

> What do you summon me for?

FORTINCOEUR

> Fortinbras is participating in battle against these pirates in six months time and he will not back down. No amount of bribery will convince him!

PRINCE NORWAY

    I will make sure that if any of Fortinbras's ships stop at Oslo to restock supplies, that no word about the tragedy will reach him. Let us hope that Fortinbras himself won't become a tragedy.

FORTINCOEUR

    This is ridiculous. Why can't we just tell him about the tragedy instead of setting all this up? It can't possibly work forever.

PRINCE NORWAY

    Do you want to be the reason your son fails as king and Denmark falls?

FORTINCOEUR

    It won't happen that way…

PRINCE NORWAY

    Do you want to try it? Do you want to be the one everyone in Denmark blames when their lives are ruined? Do you want your son to be reviled when he fails as king?

FORTINCOEUR

    No…

PRINCE NORWAY

    Then don't.

Exit Prince Norway

Exit Fortincoeur

Scene 14: *At the Swedish Castle*

At the Swedish Castle

Enter King Sweden, Messenger

MESSENGER

    Your majesty, I have news for Sweden.

KING SWEDEN

    Speak.

MESSENGER

    Recent reports in the past month are that Denmark has accelerated the building of ships, and war weapons.

KING SWEDEN

    To what purpose?

MESSENGER

    It seems to be against pirates between Denmark and Norway. I've heard whispers and predictions about how their powerful navy shall change their control on their tollways.

KING SWEDEN

    Thank you. If you have no more to say, you may leave now.

Exit Messenger

KING SWEDEN

    I cannot take the country next to us appearing to prepare for war lightly. I shall prepare our army, in case Denmark strays from their goal of eliminating these pirates. Should Denmark succeed at doing all the work and would like to increase their troublesome tolls, I must think of a way to negotiate these troubles away. I do not want their dominion over our seas.

Exit King Sweden

Scene 15: *At a large room in Elsinore castle*

At a large room in Elsinore castle

Enter crowd of castle-people for audience

Enter Fortinbras

FORTINBRAS

    I will make this speech brief. After many nights and months of toil, I am proud to announce that Denmark's new navy is finally finished! We shall set sail tomorrow to fight these pirates, and my main concerns will be on the oceans. When our battles are done, we shall control the surrounding seas. By the end of my second year of ruling, a new age of prosperity will be upon Denmark!

Audience claps.

FORTINBRAS

    While I'm away, Fortinjambes will be in charge of this kingdom. While I rather that it not happen, should I die in battle, you will appoint her as the Queen of Denmark. From all my years I have known her, having wits and energy that matches mine, I know she would make an excellent queen.

Now, let us feast!

Exit Fortinbras, audience.

Scene 16: *Grave*

Night

Hamlet's Grave

Enter Gravedigger, Horatio

GRAVEDIGGER

      Here again, to tell him of your failures over the past months? I'm going to intervene this time and actually tell you advice for once, because I've finally had too much of your melancholy. I think the children of Denmark do know the true story you are trying to spread, but they prefer stories they make.

HORATIO

      Why?

GRAVEDIGGER

      Of course a child would love to enact Mad Hamlet the Slayer, or those other strange stories! What children would not love to wave sticks around, hit their friends while saying nonsense, and watch their friends pretend to die, making the most gruesome noises and spasms a child could muster?

HORATIO

    I wish Denmark's children would not love violence so much. I've seen too much of the real thing.

GRAVEDIGGER

    Then you should thank me, for being the burier of violence, illness, and all other real horrors!

Enter Fortinbras

Horatio and the Gravedigger turn around to look at the shadowed figure

GRAVEDIGGER

    Look at that princely figure! Could it be, that Hamlet's phantom is here after all?

HORATIO

    Could it be? Hamlet? My poor prince, have you finally breached your confines and come to earth to tell me something?

Horatio reaches out to touch Fortinbras's face

HORATIO

    Your face is still warm… and different?

FORTINBRAS

    Admiring it now, are you?

GRAVEDIGGER

    To think Hamlet and Horatio could be reunited at last! And I always thought the reunion would be that Horatio would go completely mad, dig up his grave, then jump in!

HORATIO

    You absolute knave! This is the king! If I had more cruelty, and less manners, you would not need to dig your own grave because I would bury you myself!

Excuse my burst of anger. Your majesty, aren't you setting sail tomorrow? As your advisor, I prefer you would not be up so late. What brings you here?

FORTINBRAS

    Maybe to see Hamlet's grave. Maybe to see you. I know it's your habit to visit here. I see it from my window.

HORATIO

    Are you here to rebuke me? Condemn me to be a madman over my excessive grief?

FORTINBRAS

    Horatio, do you remember the time I taught you how to shoot at targets?

HORATIO

    What about it?

FORTINBRAS

    You are a surprisingly incredible marksman. You also don't fear death, since you were willing to die alongside Hamlet. Why haven't you become a soldier to fight alongside me?

HORATIO

You have come here to recruit me into the military!? I only took those shooting lessons under the guise it was merely sport. You already know I would rather not witness violence, or be the cause of it. And I don't like you enough to die alongside you anyway.

FORTINBRAS

Is that so? Good. I'm glad we're not friends, so that if I die at sea, you won't grieve for me. I apologise, for having failed as king, to make you enjoy Denmark within my time of ruling over here.

GRAVEDIGGER

Your majesty, have you stayed awake just to gossip about your feelings with your not-friend? If you die in battle tomorrow because you weren't alert, I will make sure your memorial is shaped like a bed!

FORTINBRAS

Make it a stable, so my favourite horse can mourn for me, and sleep over my grave.

Horatio, truly, I have come here to task you with exercising Mourner every day, while I'm at sea. In your room will be a map containing her usual route through the town, to the fields beyond, and near the edges of the land.

HORATIO

So that's the reason behind all those horse-riding lessons. Duly noted…

Exit everybody

Scene 17: *Elsinore shores*

Elsinore shores

Enter lots of men, boarding a ship.

Enter Fortinbras, Fortinjambes, Captain, Stable-Hand

Fortinjambes hugs Fortinbras.

FORTINJAMBES

    No pirates shall live to tell the tale of Fortinbras the Ferocious!

FORTINBRAS

    What a wonderful name! If I had the time, I'd think up more wonderful names for all the other admirals and captains.

FORTINJAMBES

    Also, surprise! I finally got you the gift. I asked a blacksmith in town to make a miniature statue of Mourner.

FORTINBRAS

    Lovely, thank you very much! I am glad that she can come into our naval battles in some form. I also have a gift for you, before I leave, and it is this set of knives. Your knife-throwing has become a lot less accurate since the last time I saw you, so while I'm away, you can entertain yourself by practising.

FORTINJAMBES

> Thank you.

STABLE-HAND

> I've brought you a gift too! It's a coat. Keep yourself warm.

FORTINBRAS

> Thank you. It's lovely! Farewell both of you, and make sure chaos does not wreak upon Denmark!

FORTINJAMBES

> Good-bye brother!

STABLE-HAND

> Good-bye and stay safe!

Exit Fortinbras, Stablehand

FORTINJAMBES

> How has it come to this? Norway's army should have wiped out most of the pirates by now then sent notice I could return. Are there really that many of them? How is it, that I've become the overseer Denmark? But I have been given this duty, and I should do her honour...

Exit Fortinjambes

Scene 18: *At the Elsinore castle stables*

At the Elsinore castle stables

Enter Marcellus, Bernardo, Stable-hand, Horatio riding in on an invisible-horse/Whatever prop for Mourner was available

Horatio dismounts from Mourner

BERNARDO

    Horatio, you looked so handsome on that horse!

STABLE-HAND

    Yes, he gets better at riding her every day! She was unsure of him first, but within a month, she carries you as if she had always known you!

HORATIO

    Only because you've taught me well.

MARCELLUS

    You are so lucky to have the privilege of riding the king's favourite horse.

HORATIO

    It is nothing grand really, and today was rather difficult. She decided that her usual steadiness was unneeded. Aren't you two supposed be on watch?

BERNARDO

    Francisco and some other sentinels are on watch, so we have all the time to admire you and Mourner!

MARCELLUS

    Horatio, you say riding Mourner is nothing grand, but I see you have a sense of purpose in your stride now!

Walking to her stable everyday has no longer become your chore. Tell me, what is it like to be on her?

HORATIO

I didn't want to boast about riding the king's horse, but really, it's like we're flying. You feel so alive when it takes all your might to hold on. It is something I didn't expect to enjoy as much as I have.

MARCELLUS

I'm glad to hear you enjoy it. If only today weren't so cloudy, then we would be able to see her coat sparkle under the sun.

HORATIO

The clouds do concern me. They look rather menacing in their number and darkness. I think I will go inside.

Exit Horatio, Marcellus, Bernardo, Stable-Hand

Scene 19: *Somewhere inside Elsinore castle*

Somewhere inside Elsinore castle.

Enter Servant 1, Servant 2, Fortinjambes

SERVANT 1

Your highness, are you in need of anything?

FORTINJAMBES

    I want judgement of those clouds outside the window. What do you think of them?

SERVANT 1

    I don't wish to upset you.

FORTINJAMBES

    I want your honesty on those clouds, and nothing except that.

SERVANT 1

    They are horrible clouds.

SERVANT 2

    Never have I ever imagined the sky would take these colours, as if it had to peel off rotting flesh.

FORTINJAMBES

    They arrived with such speed too. Servants, give the order for everyone around the castle to come inside.

Exit Servant 1, Servant 2.

Enter Horatio, who is listlessly wandering around.

FORINTJAMBES

    Oh I am so afraid! Horatio, how much experience have you had as a royal advisor?

HORATIO

    I am sorry to inform you that I am woefully underequipped. I was only Prince Hamlet's friend, and because I was one of the witnesses of the tragedy of Elsinore, Fortinbras had made me his advisor. It was only supposed to be temporary, but he never got another one. Have you your own advisors?

FORTINJAMBES

    No. This is so awful.

HORATIO

    This sky disgusts me beyond belief. You would never suspect that this was Earth's own sky. I will go down to the castle's underground casemates. Hopefully, whatever this sky brings, cannot catch me there.

FORTINJAMBES

    I will gather everyone there.

Exit Horatio, Fortinjambes

Scene 20: *Elsinore castle casemates*

Elsinore castle casemates

Enter a crowd of the castle's people, including all the actors associated with the castle, except Stable-Hand. Low level background chatter/ miming chattering. Some actors have torches.

SERVANT 2

    Princess, are you going to make a speech?

FORTINJAMBES

>I will think about it.

NURSE 1

>Poor Fortinjambes, she looks so distressed!

DOCTOR 2

>I think we are all distressed by what is going on outside. The winds are almost roaring.

FORTINJAMBES

>It's hard not to be when some people of the town chose not to shelter in the castle…

Enter Stable-Hand

FRANCISCO

>You've really brought in some of the horses?

STABLE-HAND

>It's what Fortinbras would have wanted. I'm putting them in another room, so if they get scared, we won't get trampled.

Exit Stable-Hand

Horatio is clinging to Marcellus

MARCELLUS

>Poor Horatio. You're scared out of your wits.

DOCTOR 1

    Is Horatio alright? He has been silent ever since he has entered this room, with this horrible vacant expression that looks past all of us.

MARCELLUS

    I will look after him.

Fortinjambes puts her hand up in the air to signal silence from everyone.

FORTINJAMBES

    As we are well aware, we are in a horrid situation where King Fortinbras has yet to return, and this apocalyptic sky has appeared at horrendous speed. We shall wait here. There is nothing we can do except to say our prayers, and hope the builders of ages ago had put in their utmost care when making this castle. God save us all, and the people of Denmark.

She puts her hand down.

She starts to cry.

FORTINJAMBES

    Fortinbras is wrong, I can't deal with this.

NURSE 1

    You must, you must…

Fortinjambes and Nurse 1 sit down together. The onstage actors also sit down, while the offstage stagehands make roaring wind-noises. Some actors fall asleep.

Eventually the wind noises stop, and the actors start standing up.

MARCELLUS

    Hear, it is silent now. I'm going outside. Are you coming with me Horatio?

Horatio nods.

COURTIER 1

    Fortinbras has not returned. Fortinjambes, are you becoming queen now?

FORTINJAMBES

    No… I will wait a week or so, in case, by some miracle, he has survived.

Exit Fortinjambes, then everyone else

Scene 21: *Outside of Elsinore castle*

Outside of Elsinore castle.

Enter everyone that was huddled in the castle, and Stable-hand. They look at the sky, then ahead.

FRANCISCO

    The sky is as bright and blue as can be.

FORTINJAMBES

    You'd never believe such a gentle sky has turned people's homes, with walls strong enough to see several generations of family, into small hills of matchsticks, rubble, and blood. Doctors, nurses, do not worry for me, attend to the townspeople right away!

Exit doctors and nurses

FORTINJAMBES

    What is a princess against this horrendous power? What am I to do?

COURTIER 1

    In some way, you must lead society to rebuild their houses, and regrow their food.

HORATIO

    How can we rebuild our society when the peasants are dead? The people who have worked their entire life for Denmark and made the food we eat, died thanklessly in their weak homes.

MARCELLUS

    Horatio, there are survivors, crawling out of the cracks! As long as they are there, a part of Denmark will remember them.

HORATIO

    Marcellus, and anyone with strength, come with me! I dread looking at the dead, but what I dread more is abandoning those who could have lived.

Exit Horatio, Marcellus, Francisco, Bernardo, Courtier 1, some other castle people

FORTINJAMBES

    Messengers, survey the land, and come back to me with a report on the damage on Denmark.

Exit messengers.

STABLE-HAND

    Look, look! There are wrecked ships at the ports and men rising from the sea!

Enter Fortinbras, Captain, several soldiers

FORTINJAMBES

    You're alive! But… how? How did you survive this… horrendous thing?

She gestures to the sky

FORTINBRAS

    One clear night, while I was on the deck, the warm air almost froze to ice. Then I saw an illuminated woman, that looked much like yourself, floating in the ocean. Her face contorted for a silent scream, then she vanished into blood. Upon seeing this horrible omen, I commanded my ship, and any ships following mine, to return to Denmark at once. The other ships elsewhere, with the other admirals, I do not know their fate, but I hope they heeded the cold air's warning.

Fortinbras looks ahead, at the town

The town… Aksel, ready any of the surviving horses, and get some rope so we can remove the rubble. Soldiers, we will go down there and search for the survivors.

Exit everyone off stage.

Scene 22: *At Elsinore town*

At Elsinore town

Enter Horatio, Marcellus, Francisco, Bernardo, a courtier, doctors, some other castle people, and some townspeople. Some are dead, some are on the ground, looking through rubble. Some doctors are treating townspeople in the background.

Horatio drags out a young townsperson out of the rubble/from the ground. Then he returns to vacantly staring.

BERNARDO

How is it that we keep recovering children?

MARCELLUS

In the chaos of these fallen buildings, there is a constant. That the parents were holding their children.

FRANCISCO

Look over there, men and their horses are arriving.

Enter Fortinbras, Captain, soldiers, with their horses

CAPTAIN

I see you men have done a fine job to have helped these people.

FRANCISCO

    You're alive!

CAPTAIN

    Our king felt the air turn cold and set our course back to Denmark immediately. I have low hopes for the other ships that were not near us.

BERNARDO

    (quietly to Marcellus) Look. Fortinbras is stunned. He has the same vacant stare that Horatio has right now.

CAPTAIN

    Your majesty?

Fortinbras stops staring.

FORTINBRAS

    Are there pieces of the town that you believe are covering people? We will move them with our horses.

TOWNSPERSON

    This way.

Captain, Soldiers and Fortinbras almost move offstage, but is blocked by an Old Townsperson.

OLD TOWNSPERSON

    You wretched villain!

FORTINBRAS

    Please move aside.

OLD TOWNSPERSON

    How is Denmark going to recover from this? You talked my son and the sons of many, into fighting at sea, only to have this storm sink them all to watery graves! Who will look after these children? Who will rebuild these houses? Who will work the farms?

FORTINBRAS

    I repeat my request that you step aside.

Old Townsperson tries to punch Fortinbras, but he catches the Old Townsperson's arm. Old Townsperson struggles, but Fortinbras does not let go.

OLD TOWNSPERSON

    Unhand me you crowned swine! You demon! You plague upon Denmark!

Horatio steps in between them.

HORATIO

    You two, enough! Are we, or are we not, going to use these horses?

Fortinbras releases Old Townsperson.

FORTINBRAS

    We will go.

Exit everyone.

Scene 23: *Fortinbras's quarters*

Night

Fortinbras's quarters

Enter Fortinbras

FORTINBRAS

     How had the bloodshed at town stopped me today, when a few days earlier, we were shooting pirate ships and plunging our swords into their bodies? I can't be ineffectual now, my heart should be hardened against seeing bloody affairs. Even so, that old townsperson bothers me long after having left. There were no lies in those words. I sent my people to die, children will grow without their fathers like I did, and Denmark suffers for it.

Has living in Denmark, with no thoughts of avenging anyone, softened me so much? No, I cannot stop and mourn for everyone…I cannot. I cannot. I –

Enter Fortinjambes, Doctor 1, Doctor 2, Horatio, Captain

Somebody knocks at the door. Fortinbras opens it.

FORTINBRAS

     Never knew I had such a large audience! How long have you all been waiting for, and what is your business?

FORTINJAMBES

     We've just arrived.

DOCTOR 1

     Your majesty, are you well?

FORTINBRAS

I am! Begone all you doctors!

Exit doctors

FORTINJAMBES

We're here to inquire what you shall do tomorrow. Have you received the messengers' reports?

FORTINBRAS

Yes, and I've done some surveying of the land around Elsinore myself. Our population, buildings, crops, ships, destroyed or halved.

The situation is troubling. Even with the reduced amount of people, I don't think the amount of food we have left will be able to provide for Denmark long enough to wait for the new crops to grow. We will have to acquire food from Sweden, the north side of that country may be spared from the storm.

CAPTAIN

Our wealth was depleted when building all those ships. While we might be able to import some food from Sweden, I don't believe we have enough money to feed Denmark long enough to live off what is left, and for new food to grow. Denmark cannot increase its wealth with all the reduced people, nor with no crops to export. For our income, we are relying on the Sound tollway.

FORTINBRAS

The Sound tollway has been an extremely reliable source of income, but I am doubtful of the amount of ships that will be sailing through here after the cursed sky swept the seas. Then… I absolutely hate to say it, but I will become Sweden's beggar, and I will beg in the flesh to their king, to make it more convincing. I am cornered, and I would rather not watch my countrymen slowly starve to death. Tomorrow, we will begin our journey to the Tre Kronor castle, in Stockholm.

CAPTAIN

How many men would you like to accompany you?

Fortinbras hands him a paper

FORTINBRAS

I've written our planned route and other considerations on this paper. I hope it should be enough to carry supplies and fight off any thieves or other unruly men. Gather everything right away, since we're leaving on short notice.

FORTINJAMBES

Can I come? If my brother is begging, so am I. I want to help Denmark.

FORTINBRAS

Someone will need to oversee Denmark while we're away. You can help in that position.

HORATIO

I support Fortinjambe's desire to come to Sweden. She can play on the sympathies of the Swedish king if she cries in front of him.

FORTINJAMBES

I quite like Horatio's idea.

FORTINBRAS

I relent, she can come if she could increase our chances of Sweden helping us. I will ask someone else to oversee Denmark.

FORTINJAMBES

I will practise tonight! Though it hardly needs practice, since Denmark is in such a bad state…

Exit Fortinjambes

FORTINBRAS

You're going to Sweden too, Horatio. If my begging fails, and the king is not moved by her womanly weeping, you and the Captain will try negotiating with him.

CAPTAIN

Any more people?

FORTINBRAS

No.

Exit Captain

FORTINBRAS

Horatio, Horatio, I was unwise to ignore your words of advice months earlier, about not fighting against the pirates. How could you ever forgive me?

HORATIO

It is not my forgiveness that you should be seeking.

FORTINBRAS

Yes. I know Denmark will never forgive me. I can never bring back their lost men in the sea. You're probably one of the few people in this entire country who possibly could forgive me, because you are still alive, and had no close relatives die from a result of my decision.

HORATIO

Then that possibility is gone. I had enjoyed riding Mourner, out to see parts of Denmark, and now my joy is gone. The people I saw are dead. My memories are located at graveyards now. Denmark is now not just your father's grave, its land and people have become a memorial to those that you sent to die at sea.

FORTINBRAS

Horatio, I didn't mean for Denmark to become a graveyard for everyone else too. How was I supposed to know that this sudden storm would kill all these men?

HORATIO

If you're begging for forgiveness, please leave your begging to the Swedish King. Good-bye Fortinbras. If you don't dismiss me tomorrow, I will accompany you on your journey in Sweden.

Horatio goes outside the room, closes the door/ to the edge of the stage. Horatio does not exit.

Fortinbras goes to his window to puke/retch

FORTINBRAS

      Expunge yourself, horrible feeling growing within me. How foolish was I, trying to justify myself to Horatio. He knows my own reasons for doing what I did, and that I only had good intentions for Denmark. If he cannot understand my reasons, those limitations are his. I had done the same thing as I had done before, as a prince, and as many other princes do, when we go and fight. The only difference this time was the result, which was the fault of nature, not mine. Had this storm not appeared, even if a few men had died while fighting pirates, if a majority came back and Denmark enjoyed the spoils of the battles, no one would have fault with what I had decided.

Fortinbras sits near the window.

HORATIO

      And so, in this moment, he has cleared his guilty conscience. The deaths of many men that he had taken part in causing, do not hang upon his mind for more than a week. Yet, with Hamlet's death, which I did not stop when I had some doubts about this fencing wager with Laertes, will haunt me for the rest of my life, though Hamlet chose to go to it. The grief and guilt from the over a year-ago Elsinore tragedy is a curse that left me stagnant, but now I feel it is better to be filled with it than to force those feelings out of the body early with those retches. Blocking his emotion by reasoning that those deaths that he took part in were supposed to be, and his habit of leaving his horse to feel mournful instead of him… Hamlet pondered death heavily and felt he must face Laertes for his wrongs against him. What life has Fortinbras lived, to have practised this clearing of horrors from his mind at utmost speed?

Exit Horatio

Exit Fortinbras

Scene 24: *Shores of Poland*

Shores of Poland

Enter Polish Prince, and a pirate (lying on the floor)

POLISH PRINCE

    All these shipwrecks and bodies upon the shores of Poland, what has been going on?

PIRATE

    Down here! Look down here!

POLISH PRINCE

    Stranger, what brings you flailing on beach?

PIRATE

    I was a pirate, but now I've sustained enough injury that there's not enough life in me left to live another day. Denmark's navy had killed nearly all of us, but something had killed nearly all of Denmark's navy.

POLISH PRINCE

    What has shattered Denmark's navy here?

PIRATE

    Unearthly winds strong enough to turn the heavens. If your nation has anything against Denmark, now or anytime soon is the time to do it. I'm certain the winds have left their country in shambles.

POLISH PRINCE

(To the pirate) May God take care of you, lost soul.

(To himself) Poland has felt some of these winds, which had wrecked some of our own ships and felled a few houses, but not strong enough to mix all these splinters into the sand.

It is true, Poland does have grudges against Denmark. First Old Hamlet came here to slay us, and the current Danish king slew some of us over a small piece of land while he was the Prince of Norway.

When Poland has recovered from the wind's damage, I will take this opportunity to show Denmark that Poland will not be trampled on.

Exit Pirate, Polish Prince

Scene 25: *Helsingborg*

Helsingborg

Enter Fortinbras, Fortinjambes, Captain, Horatio, several soldiers, departing a small boat. Characters are taking supplies off.

FORTINJAMBES

How lucky we are, that you wanted a few of these small boats and ships to be built, and the castle shielded them from the winds. We would never make it across the Sound Strait on our way to Sweden otherwise.

FORTINBRAS

My arms may be strong, but I never want to participate in making several trips to row horses and supplies across the strait ever again. If I'm glad for anything, it would be for this ship's sails that lightened the work considerably.

SOLDIER

Did I miss another announcement early in the morning? If the king is here, the princess is here, then who's in charge of the kingdom?

FORTINBRAS

A stable-hand, the sentinels, and that sailing captain that arrived with Fortinjambes.

SOLDIER

Really? Why did you pick those ordinary people?

FORTINBRAS

It makes no difference at this point. One is my lifelong friend from Norway, the other is an acquaintance, and the rest are Danes. If someone wanted to invade at this time, I doubt any money a noble had could bribe the invaders away, and the amount of experience you have in commanding an army can't amount to anything if there barely is an army. I've sent most of the surviving men back to their homes to assist their people. If a few merchants with food arrive on our shores, the people I've appointed have all my permission to spend whatever is left of Denmark's money.

FORTINJAMBES

There's not much difference between us and an ordinary person anyway, when it comes to being sensible. It's the amount of responsibility that separates us. Take an ordinary person, give them an immense amount of responsibility, and if the person takes the challenge, they could soon turn out just like my brother, or me.

FORTINBRAS

Yes.

(to a few soldiers, but not all of them) Take this boat back to the castle, and look after that boat at Helsingborg in case we will need it on the way back.

Exit everyone.

Scene 26: *Scania, Denmark*

Scania, Denmark

Enter Fortinbras, Fortinjambes, Captain, Horatio, several soldiers.

HORATIO

How horrible to see, that the storm has reached this far east into Scania. Death is unescapable, with bodies all the way here…

CAPTAIN

    I've yet to see Denmark's west, but I wouldn't be surprised if the storm had perused all of Denmark and left no space unturned. Nature's power is beyond anything that can be witnessed on a battlefield.

FORTINBRAS

    To see my kingdom covered in cracked trees, split houses, and the occasional sight of a human impaled, they're needles to my eyes…

Enter a Dane

A DANE

    Please sirs, I'm begging you. I see you all have some food, while we have lost most of ours during the storm.

CAPTAIN

    Fortinbras?

Pause

FORTINBRAS

    Horatio?

HORATIO

    [aside] Pass this decision onto me? Has he been suddenly struck with newfound cowardice, or does he trust me?

We have a few turnips you can take.

A DANE

>How many?

HORATIO

>As many as you think is right.

The Dane takes five turnips.

A DANE

>Thank you very much! God bless your soul!

The Dane runs off. All the other soldiers stare at Horatio.

HORATIO

>What would you all have said?! If you dislike it, then I will face the consequences and skip five turnips worth in meals.

FORTINBRAS

>Horatio's decision had been made, and five turnips it was. If he starts starving to death, then we will have pity on him.

Exit everyone.

Scene 27: *Close to Stockholm*

Close to Stockholm

Enter Fortinbras, Fortinjambes, Captain, Horatio, several soldiers

CAPTAIN

That most southern section of Sweden looked quite like Denmark. Equally horrible. At least it appears Sweden has been mostly spared from this storm.

FORTINBRAS

I can see Stockholm ahead of us. Damn this entire quest! If there is doom, I will walk into it because I feel I must, but no amount of obligation will make me hate it less!

FORTINJAMBES

What are you riled up for?

FORTINBRAS

The moment I go in and beg, there disappears the last of my honour. If Denmark somehow survives to become prosperous, the Swedes will be passing on down tales of Fortinbras the Beggar for the rest of my life, and years beyond it! The king could also refuse all our begging, and we'd have performed as jesters for free.

What if we went in there, and vanquished the Swedish king by surprise? I'd control Sweden, which will let me send help to Denmark, then this entire cursed ordeal can be over!

FORTINJAMBES

Yes, perhaps the Swedish King can substitute for our missed chance against Old Hamlet! Should he be sliced by your sword, my knives, or the combined weapons of our entire party?

HORATIO

    Rest your wild imaginations. They would have more guards in that castle than our small party. If you killed him, the Swedes would return us the favour. Perhaps you will find it within yourself to negotiate using neither blades nor bullets. I also supported bringing Fortinjambes for this purpose of tempering any of your impulses, since I doubted you would dare risk her...

FORTINJAMBES

    I have many charming qualities, but bringing reason to people isn't one of them!

FORTINBRAS

    I will take a pause, to savour the last moments of my dignity, then we will enter Stockholm.

Pause

Exit everyone.

Scene 28: *Tre Kronor Castle*

Tre Kronor Castle

Enter King Sweden, and various Swedish guards.

Enter Fortinbras, Fortinjambes, Captain, Horatio, several soldiers

KING SWEDEN

    King Fortinbras, I've awaited for your pitiful invasion to arrive here.

FORTINBRAS

How did you know ahead of time?

KING SWEDEN

Surveyors that I've sent south have spotted your little group. What have you arrived here for?

FORTINBRAS

Recently, an utmost horrendous storm has hit Denmark, and destroyed majority of our food and crops. Tell your merchants that it's currently safe to sail down Denmark. There are no warships and pirates, and we will buy all the food, and possibly the ships themselves, that our wealth can allow.

KING SWEDEN

Pause, as the King Sweden leans in to look at Fortinbras's face.

You don't hide it well enough. Your face betrays a sense of dread. You have more to say!

Pause

FORTINBRAS

Our wealth won't be enough to feed all of Denmark until the crops regrow. Is there anything else we can do in return for food?

KING SWEDEN

Nothing.

FORTINBRAS

Nothing?

KING SWEDEN

You can do nothing. I've heard about the state of Denmark from people in Sweden's south, who had suffered the same fate as them. Everything in Denmark is wrecked, and your men are dead. You have nothing to offer, not even your wretched land and its people. I already have to worry about Sweden's south, you Danes will be a burden to us. Speak no more.

FORTINJAMBES

[weeping] Oh please, great Swedish King! This storm has devasted us so horrendously! You must understand how much pain we are in, since you have looked upon the south of your country! With all the kindness in your heart, save us from starvation and send us food, until Denmark can support itself! You will be in our eternal gratitude!

KING SWEDEN

[*He laughs.*]

So you've even brought a woman to beg for you! Fortinbras, if you were here to beg, you should do it yourself! I will hear from nobody else, except from him.

FORTINBRAS

Then I beg of you, lend us aid!

KING SWEDEN

    You stand too tall for a beggar. The rest of you, look at him, and etch this rare sight into your memory! It is not every day you see a king become a beggar! Fortinbras, on your knees!

Pause

KING SWEDEN

    On your knees.

Fortinbras goes to his knees.

KING SWEDEN

    And you are too armed for a beggar as well. Guards, take his sword and hand it to me.

Fortinbras's sword is taken away by the guards and they give it to King Sweden. King Sweden inspects the sword.

KING SWEDEN

    A rather ordinary sword. For your sword, I will give you this.

The King pulls a single little coin out of his pocket, and flicks it towards Fortinbras.

KING SWEDEN

    Go on. Take your payment. You are in no position to be choose.

Fortinbras takes the coin.

FORTINBRAS

    Enough of this! Will you help us? Most of your country has been spared from the storm, and you have enough money, from all the timber we purchased.

KING SWEDEN

    Ah, yes. Timber for your navy, so Denmark can further bother us on the seas, and make us pay more for your tollway! Perhaps it was better to save Denmark's money, or invest it in something else.

FORTINBRAS

    I will remove any tolls for Sweden!

KING SWEDEN

    I'm not so unkind to take away a great source of income for Denmark in your time of need. You can keep it.

FORTINBRAS

    You can have some of our land.

KING SWEDEN

    No. I already said I would refuse it earlier. It will be a liability for us to defend.

FORTINBRAS

    Denmark will take on a debt and pay you back.

KING SWEDEN

    I'm not going to subject your citizens to even more tax after you spent their money on building Denmark's navy.

FORTINBRAS

    Then what do you want?! Because I don't want my people to starve!

KING SWEDEN

    You, a band of Danish beggars, asking me for what I want? You'd be adorable if you weren't so pathetic. They have yet to fall, but I can see your eyes have reddened from tears, young Fortinbras. Well, I'd like for you to leave me alone. This storm has troubled Sweden's south enough, Denmark's tollway has troubled Sweden enough, and we don't need to have anything to do with you.

But for this entertainment, I will comply with sending out the notice that it is safe to sail to Denmark.

Give our temporary jesters some food so we don't have to bury their bodies on Swedish land. Prepare a merchant ship, and ship these and their horses back to Denmark. If they wish to have the ship and its contents, they can pay for it upon reaching Elsinore. We will have another smaller ship accompany the merchant ship, for carrying money and whatever isn't bought back to Sweden.

Exit everyone

Scene 29: *Ship*

Swedish Merchant ship

Enter Fortinbras, Fortinjambes, Captain, Horatio, several soldiers, and the Swedish merchant who is sailing the ship

SOLDIER

    Since the start of our journey home, each morning has turned our king into a statue, devoted to staring at the sea, until night.

CAPTAIN

    Sometimes he does that. Let him be.

FORTINJAMBES

    I'm glad our journey back must be nearly over by now. We had journeyed all the way to Sweden, and our begging was for naught! How horrible! Horatio and the Captain couldn't even get a word in!

HORATIO

    If it brings you any joy, at least we have this large ship and all its contents once we buy it, and we can sail elsewhere. Perhaps Norway will be kinder.

FORTINJAMBES

    I will demand it! My uncle cannot refuse, and if he does, he is worth nothing. I would take his crown if that would help Denmark.

HORATIO

    It seems forming strange schemes is a shared family trait…

Fortinbras begins puking/retching

HORATIO

    [aside] And so he purges whatever inhabited so much of his body, that lead him to stillness.

SOLDIER

    Is the king alright? It is a shame to have scant food at Denmark, and to see the king lose his from where it should stay in.

CAPTAIN

    The previous times I've seen this, he always tells me it's just sea-sickness, and to leave him alone. I pity him. To be such an experienced sailor, and still suffer from sea-sickness!

Everyone pauses as they watch the sea

CAPTAIN

    Horatio, I am glad you are here.

HORATIO

    Why?

CAPTAIN

    I saw you helping the townspeople after the storm, and then you had given up food for yourself so easily. After seeing that scene at the Swedish castle, it is nice to have moments of kindness in my memory.

HORATIO

    I only did what I should. How could I refuse, after looking into the eyes of someone who needed help? A cost to me that truly benefits someone helpless, I will bear through that pain.

FORTINBRAS

I can attest to Horatio's character. His dedication to others, especially Hamlet, with nary a thought to himself. I'm surprised he's still with us.

HORATIO

I share that same surprise.

CAPTAIN

I do not understand what this is, about Horatio not having yet disappeared, but I assume it's a joke between you two. I'm glad to see you're well again, my lord.

FORTINBRAS

There is no lord beside you.

CAPTAIN

Then who is beside me?

FORTINBRAS

Horatio and a disgrace.

FORTINJAMBES

Cheer up brother. If the Swedish king is going to spread tales about Fortinbras the Beggar, I'm going to spread tales about Sweden the Selfish!

Look! Is that Elsinore over there? I hope it is. This sudden chill bothers me greatly.

Pause

Fortinbras? Your knuckles are white.

FORTINBRAS

    I pray to every heavenly power that I'm mistaken, and it is instead a slight effect of the weather. But this sudden rush of cold air, it was the same I felt before I saw the bad omen in the sea that preceded the storm. Elsinore is near. When we have reached the shores, buy the ship from the merchant, beach it, and tether every part of it. Take its contents to the castle. We will also beach and tether any of the smaller ships.

Exit everyone.

Scene 30: *Somewhere in Elsinore Castle*

Somewhere in Elsinore Castle.

Enter Servant 1, Servant 2

SERVANT 1

    The clouds devouring the skies are so thick, that the daytime has almost become as dark as night.

SERVANT 2

    What is going on!? Why is this happening again? Denmark is already devastated. If this is more of the same, there will be nothing of Denmark left!

Enter Stable-Hand, with the horses

SERVANT 1

    If only I was a horse! I could just eat grass all day and worry less about the weather.

STABLE-HAND

You should pick a different wish. I knew something was wrong because the horses were acting strangely.

SERVANT 2

Is it the same strangeness as when that horrible wind blew us over?

STABLE-HAND

It is similar, but different.

Enter Courtier 1

COURTIER 1

The king has given orders for everyone to avoid the casemates! There's water leaking in it.

Exit everyone

Scene 31: *Middle floors of the castle*

Middle floors of castle

Enter Servant 1, Servant 2, Courtier 1, Fortinbras

SERVANT 2

Are you sure that the king was the one that gave the orders? All I see is that he is staring out of the window, softly laughing to himself, as if the further destruction of Denmark is a mere passing amusement!

COURTIER 1

    The very same person.

Fortinbras stops laughing and turns to look at the servants and courtiers.

SERVANT 1

    I think I will stand on another floor.

Exit Servant 1, Servant 2, Courtier 1

Fortinbras looks out of the window again.

Enter Stable-Hand

STABLE-HAND

    I've put the horses in the castle's bottom floor.

FORTINBRAS

    Thank you.

Stable Hand walks closer to Fortinbras

STABLE-HAND

    I can see that you're unwell now. If there is anything I can do to help, please, tell me.

Enter Horatio.

FORTINBRAS

    A mere stable-hand, or a king, cannot do anything about the sky pouring blood! The gall of the heavens! To be over a year-late to warn Denmark of what Claudius was doing!

I jest. These presents from heaven are for me. God knows I've wasted lives on that useless scrap of land in Poland. And God knows I've wasted even more from fighting the pirates.

Look at this man in front of you. His parents' lands have become nothing but a drowned pile of wind-swept mud. A son with no dignity of his own, a mere beggar, surrounded by a graveyard of his own making. Witness Denmark bleeding, because of me.

STABLE-HAND

There is only water falling outside. While these storms are freakish and utterly strange, I don't think this is divine punishment on you. Otherwise every other country with a prince that goes into battle would be plagued by these storms.

FORTINBRAS

I cannot think of another explanation. And this is why I must never be idle! My idleness leads to straying thoughts, which shall paralyse me the more I ponder them, which leads to more idleness and pondering! Idleness within me festers. I hate this rain, forcing me to stand in this castle and watch it smother Denmark, turning its dreamlike landscape into a nightmare.

Exit Fortinbras

STABLE-HAND

Horatio, you were here?

HORATIO

    I was going to pass to an upper floor, but the conversation captured my interest.

STABLE-HAND

    Please don't tell the doctors. I know the situation is dire, but the doctors force him into idleness in hopes it will pass. Instead, it begets more situations similar to what you have heard.

HORATIO

    You speak as if these situations have happened before.

STABLE-HAND

    Only when he was a child, from grief over his father, and a few times when he was older. He has handled himself well as an adult.

HORATIO

    Does anyone need to keep watch on him?

STABLE-HAND

    He only likes being watched when he wants to be watched.

HORATIO

    I understand.

[aside] To go mad from being idle, or to be reckless from constantly moving. His efforts had not stopped his guilt piling up. Does this cursed existence lie in my future?

Exit Horatio, Stable-Hand

Scene 32: *Another floor of Elsinore Castle*

Another floor of Elsinore Castle

Enter Marcellus, Bernardo, Francisco, Captain, Horatio, Fortinjambes, several doctors. They're sitting.

BERNARDO

    How awful. There are people out there, having their crops and whatever is left of their homes washed away, and we're in here, playing cards, and eating food from that Swedish ship.

FRANCISCO

    I'm afraid to see what remains of Denmark. Within the span of a few months, much of what us Danes have built over decades has disintegrated.

MARCELLUS

    There were somehow survivors of the previous storm, and I believe there will be survivors of this torrential downpour. I'm amazed that we small people have survived, against those immense forces of fortune and nature.

CAPTAIN

    We told Sweden that the waters near Denmark are safe for their merchants to sail to, and if any had listened to us, now they surely must be getting sunk by all this rain!

HORATIO

    Sometimes I regret living all the way until now. Mostly I've been rewarded with horrid events, and I never know when they will end.

FORTINJAMBES

    You'd be surprised by how many things also happen to be in the right place at the right time… Hopefully, your continued existence will be the latter.

Enter Fortinbras, dragging a sword along the ground

BERNARDO

    Oh, like that! Francisco just lost, and we have a new player to replace him in our card game.

FORTINJAMBES

    (to doctors) Is this worthy of acting upon?

DOCTOR 1

    (to Fortinjambes) A noteworthy rule is to never venture near him while he has a sword in hand.

BERNARDO

    Your majesty, do you want to play cards with us? You seem rather bored.

MARCELLUS

    What is going on with him?

HORATIO

    I've been told he hates being idle. Let him be.

Fortinbras stops walking.

FORTINBRAS

 Captain, after we have given some of the castle's food to the townspeople at Elsinore, we will have some men inspect the merchant ship for its seaworthiness, remove any excess bilge water, and hopefully no major repairs will be needed. From the windows, I can see that our efforts to beach and tether it have served it well. We will sail to Norway once we can, and ask for help. Fortinjambes, and if they wish, the other Norwegians that came with her, will be aboard the ship to be returned to Norway. You, Horatio, and perhaps one of the sentinels will also come. The rest of the ship will be for supplies.

HORATIO

 What do you need me for? I doubt your negotiations for help from Norway will be difficult. It's your own family.

MARCELLUS

 I will go, but I don't know what I will be doing either.

FORTINBRAS

 The vastness of the sea can play on the minds of people. You two Danes can keep each other reasonable while we sail there.

HORATIO

 I don't understand. You wouldn't need to bring two Danes to keep each other reasonable, if you bring none of us.

FORTINBRAS

(to Horatio) Family negotiations can sometimes be complicated, and I can tell Aksel chose to speak to you.

Francisco and Bernardo, I once again leave you in charge of Denmark when I set sail, along with the stable-hand named Aksel. I trust that you will distribute the food sensibly.

FRANCISCO

We will.

Exit everyone.

Scene 34: *Elsinore Town*

Elsinore Town

Enter Peasant 1, Peasant 2, Townsperson 1, Townsperson 2

PEASANT 1

After the windstorm, I spent so much time putting new seeds into the ground, and now I have nothing but drenched dirt to eat after this rainstorm! What is there left to do apart from starve and die? No one from any other country will want to sail to Denmark and give us their food, with all these disasters around us.

TOWNSPERSON 1

Listen, what if all these disasters are to do with the king? Think about it. Before he ruled, he wanted to kill Old

Hamlet, then Old Hamlet had died in the most horrific way, being killed by his own family! When Fortinbras arrived in Denmark, Claudius, Hamlet, Gertrude, Laertes died on that same day. While Fortinbras ruled, in less than two years, his fanciful words of prosperity took our men's minds and murdered them at sea, and Denmark has been swept by two storms. Fortinbras and some higher power must be involved to let all these disasters happen.

PEASANT 2

      Yes, he does seem to bring death where he goes. I wouldn't be surprised if he was somehow a demon sent to kill everyone in Denmark. There's not much difference between how a demon sent to vanquish us, and what he has done during his rule, would do.

TOWNSPERSON 2

      If he is the root from which Denmark's doom springs from, then we must weed him out! I will grab whatever tools I have, and you others grab yours. We've nothing to lose but our inevitable loss of life from Fortinbras ruling, and Denmark to gain!

PEASANT 1

      I will ask the priest to bless my tools, to make sure whatever evil power inhabiting Fortinbras will be conquered if I strike him!

Exit peasants and townspeople

Enter Fortinbras, Captain, Soldiers, all with their horses, Marcellus, Horatio (not on a horse)

CAPTAIN

    People of Elsinore! We have brought you food, to relieve you from suffering momentarily! There is no need to pay for it!

Pause

HORATIO

    I came here to see if anyone needed help, but a horrible silence greets our ears.

MARCELLUS

    Where is everyone? Did no one truly survive that second storm?

FORTINBRAS

    That can't be. While the rains were strong and have done considerable damage to the farms and some buildings, they weren't as powerful as the windstorm. Surely there must be some people left…

Enter peasants and townspeople with weapons

PEASANT 1

    Kill the demon!

TOWNSPERSON 1

    Take his head!

The soldiers pull their swords and stop the townspeople

PEASANT 2

    Wretched creature! You dare have soldiers attacking your own subjects?

TOWNSPERSON 2

    He wants us Danes to die!

The mob grows bigger, the soldiers have difficulty with holding them back. Fortinbras pulls his sword out. Horatio begins backing away.

HORATIO

    Fortinbras, leave!

A townsperson manages to strike Fortinbras's horse/the Mourner prop.

Fortinbras exits.

MARCELLUS

    Horatio, go after him! We'll quell these people!

Exit Horatio

Exit everyone else

Scene 35: *An empty field at the edge of Denmark*

An empty field at the edge of Denmark.

Enter Fortinbras

FORTINBRAS

    My poor Mourner, your running has brought us all the way here. Now your breathing is laboured, your coat shines from your own blood, and your legs are weakening. That strike was meant for me, but it is you who is in agony, you who always bore my pain throughout your life. I can see you will die, and I don't want to prolong it. Good-bye Mourner. You need not your strength, this time I will do the mourning and bear my pains instead. Turn your head, so your last memory is the beauty of the sea.

Fortinbras swings his sword, the Mourner prop drops to the ground.

FORTINBRAS

    And so she loses her head.

Fortinbras cries. He looks up for a moment.

FORTINBRAS

    A rainbow? After this rainstorm? God, do you mock me?

Enter a Rabbit, emerging from a bush.

FORTINBRAS

    What foul rabbit, who has survived multiple storms, dares hunger for her body?

RABBIT

    It is not for any body I hunger.

FORTINBRAS

    What strange powers does Denmark have, to have horrendous storms and talking rabbits?

RABBIT

    I do have strange powers to offer you. First, lower yourself so I may hear you better, and look at your face to judge your honesty.

FORTINBRAS

    Must I go to my knees again?

RABBIT

    You do not have to.

Fortinbras crouches

RABBIT

    Do you despise your subjects for what they did, hurting your horse in the attempt to kill you, when months ago, Horatio rode into town and she was their everyday joy?

FORTINBRAS

    Inside me, is a searing rage for their actions, but I do not despise my subjects. I have done nothing good for Denmark, and they are at the end of their desperation. They feel they must not be idle, and take action to help themselves. So the action is against me, who spent Denmark's wealth and their men's lives for naught, whose powers at helping them during times of devastation has not amounted to much, when helping them is my duty as king. Have our positions swapped, and I would do the same.

If there is anything, instead, I want peace for my subjects. No storms, plenty of food for everyone to eat and to grow happily, homes for them to live in. Then their anger will cease.

RABBIT

    I can promise this sort of peace to your subjects. I will use my powers to ensure that prosperity will be on these lands you now rule, for as long as you live.

In exchange, promise me your soul.

FORTINBRAS

    I do not know whether you are an angel, demon, or some other unearthly spirit, but at this point I do not care. Take my wretched soul. What is the inevitable damnation of my one useless soul, if it means all my subjects can live a long good life?

RABBIT

    The deal is done.

Exit the rabbit, disappearing into the bush.

Act 2:

Enter Horatio

HORATIO

    I have tracked Mourner's footprints and found you…Mourner, she is dead.

FORTINBRAS

    I killed her to put her at peace.

HORATIO

    That poor soul…She had brought me such joy.

They look at Mourner.

HORATIO

    Why were you talking with a rabbit?

FORTINBRAS

The rabbit itself could talk. In exchange for my soul, it said that using its strange powers, "prosperity will be on these lands I now rule, for as long as I live".

Pause

HORATIO

You damned fool! You sighted man, blind to your future consequences! You, who has cabbages-for-brains rolling down a hill, stopping at nothing! What have you done!? The town was decrying you as a demon, and now you have actually enlisted a demon's power to help you! Nothing good ever happens from dealing with a demon! Hamlet trusted you, and now his kingdom is given up to someone who thinks through nothing! If I could redo the past, I'd have told Hamlet's story, then reached for that poisoned cup again, or stuck a sword through my heart, so I could never bear witness to your foolishness! Your foolishness and the hell I will go to for killing myself, the amount of pain is the same! Your presence makes me wish my presence never were.

FORTINBRAS

Horatio, look into my eyes. I don't care if that rabbit was a demon. My power has come to almost nothing, and it's the same for my subjects. If the pain of my damnation will let them live in happiness, I will go through it. I'm sorry that I've upset you. Please don't leave.

HORATIO

You pathetic man. I also spoke too quickly. Every part of you makes me wish I could tear my own body into a mist, but I will endure living, so that we may bring Denmark peace. From now, until these problems linked to your rule over Denmark are resolved, I shall dedicate my life to watching over you, and making sure you don't bring my homeland any more trouble.

FORTINBRAS

    I accept your help. Thank you. Now, swear upon my sword, that you will never speak of this rabbit's deal to anyone else, ever. I don't want to be killed for demonic contact.

HORATIO

    This situation is all too familiar. I swear that I will never speak of the rabbit's deal to another soul. Now, about that rabbit, where did it go?

FORTINBRAS

    In the bush.

Horatio checks the bush.

HORATIO

    The bush contains nothing… If you quoted the rabbit exactly, then its words concern me.

FORTINBRAS

    I have. Explain.

HORATIO

    It could be equivocating. Prosperity will be on these lands you now rule, for as long as you live… What if you die Fortinbras?

FORTINBRAS

    Then the demon's power of apparent prosperity will no longer be upon this kingdom. My death could bring worse doom than Denmark has already endured… And my subjects are already trying to kill me. Horatio, I am a fool. Fortinbras the Fool.

HORATIO

    Fortinbras the flighty fool who thinks fully-formed thoughts fleetingly.

FORTINBRAS

    Aye. Your scholar's wit is doing you good.

Enter Marcellus

MARCELLUS

    So the footprints have lead me here. The townspeople have eased down when we finally gave them the food, told them that Horatio and other Danes had ran Fortinbras out, and that the Danes, Francisco and Bernardo, are in charge. I spotted you two, and it seemed you were arguing over something, what was it?

Marcellus spots Mourner's beheaded corpse.

FORTINBRAS

    I had to do it, she was in too much pain and wouldn't live. It came as a great shock to Horatio.

HORATIO

    Poor Mourner, we loved her so much. Seeing her death was a horrid affair, but it was better quick than to be tortured over hours.

MARCELLUS

    It's unfortunate that I didn't bring a shovel, so that we may bury her.

FORTINBRAS

    We've not much time anyway. We should get back to the ship. If nothing on it had broken, it will be ready for sail. I don't want to keep everyone else waiting. I'll mark this spot, so that we can return here to give Mourner the full respects she deserves.

Fortinbras marks the floor, near the bush, with his sword.

Exit Fortinbras, Horatio, Marcellus.

Scene 36: *Outside of Elsinore castle*

Outside Elsinore castle

Enter Fortinbras, Horatio, Marcellus

MARCELLUS

    Since when did we have so many ships? Look at them, coming to shore.

HORATIO

    Is this help for us?

Enter a bunch of Swedish soldiers

SWEDISH SOLDIER

    Are any of you King Fortinbras?

FORTINBRAS

    No.

SWEDISH SOLDIER

Takes a closer look at his face

    Ah, so you are consistent, because you're Fortinbras the beggar! I saw you beg in front of the king! Surround him and take his castle!

Swedish soldiers surround Fortinbras. Fortinbras pulls out his sword.

FORTINBRAS

    I will fight to defend Denmark with the last powers I have!

Horatio stands between them.

FORTINBRAS

    Horatio, what are you doing? Don't put your life in such peril! Have some value for yourself!

HORATIO

    No, you will not fight to defend Denmark! Have you forgotten the rabbit!?

MARCELLUS

    The rabbit?

HORATIO

    Fortinbras has a pet rabbit. He has kept it a secret though until now, because he thought people would make fun of him for it.

FORTINBRAS

    And I would hate for it to be killed in this invasion of the castle. I surrender.

SWEDISH SOLDIER

    Yes, we will very much make fun of you for surrendering lands of Denmark over a pet rabbit that is no longer a secret.

MARCELLUS

    At least surrendering means he gets to keep his life.

Enter Swedish Ambassador

SWEDISH AMBASSADOR

    In the very likely case of surrender, the Swedish king has prepared a treaty for you to sign.

Fortinbras sheathes his sword, and takes the pen and paper.

FORTINBRAS

    [reading the paper] You will cede all lands east of the Sounds Strait to Sweden. You will also cede Elsinore Castle, and the Sound Tollway.

I thought he wasn't interested in our land and the tollway? What about the rest of Denmark? How did you all arrive here through all those rains?!

SWEDISH AMBASSADOR

Perhaps God blessed our king with the visions of these lands in particular belonging to Sweden, and he decided to follow it.

Does it really matter? Sign the paper.

FORTINBRAS

(to Horatio) Do you think I should sign it?

HORATIO

You've not much choice, but if you want to attempt at making any amendments, or if there's anything in Denmark you want to keep, now is the time to say it.

FORTINBRAS

I'd like to make an amendment. If you take our castle, then you'd take the money in there, leaving no money for the Danes that live west of the Sound Strait to buy food. You will take only the castle, and none of the money. I would also like for the castle's inhabitants to have at least one day to remove all their personal possessions within.

SWEDISH AMBASSADOR

None of what you have said seems to contradict what is written, as the king mentioned only the castle, and nothing about its contents. I don't want to be fighting against the Danes with what little resources we have. I'll allow it.

FORTINBRAS

It is done…

SWEDISH AMBASSADOR

    The castle is ours!

Exit all the Swedish people.

FORTINBRAS

    Marcellus, go to our ship and report if it's ready for sail. I want to speak to Francisco, Bernardo, and the stable-hand when they come out of the castle.

Exit Marcellus

HORATIO

    Here is more of that rabbit's equivocations. Back then, it said prosperity will be on these lands you now rule, the lands being what you ruled over at the time that you made the deal, but it didn't mention anything about you being the future ruler of those lands.

FORTINBRAS

    The wounds of my foolishness cut deep. My entire life, I had been training to regain these lands, and I lose it by surrender!

Enter Francisco, Bernardo, Stable-Hand

STABLE-HAND

    So, you've surrendered! Never thought I'd see this day, but I'm glad you're still here.

BERNARDO

    Are we still in charge of Denmark?

FORTINBRAS

　　Elsinore's town, and all lands west of it, are still under your command, if there is any command you could possibly do. I've made sure that the money in Elsinore castle still belongs to Denmark.

FRANCISCO

　　Are you going to Norway now?

HORATIO

　　We are, once Marcellus tells us whether our ship is sea-worthy and ready, or not.

STABLE-HAND

　　I hope seeing Norway brings you some happiness. A change from Denmark's storm-stricken muds will do you good.

FORTINBRAS

　　I hope so too. God be with you, and good luck, for you three who have to look after Denmark. If I come back here, and some other country has taken over Denmark, I won't blame you.

BERNARDO

　　Thank you.

FORTINBRAS

　　Aksel, you may take all my personal possessions within the castle. Also… Mourner has died. She was injured, and I had to put her to rest. Her body lies close to the north coast of Elsinore. If you see her, please bury her…

The Stable-Hand hugs Fortinbras.

STABLE-HAND

    I will.

Exit Stable-Hand, Bernardo, Francisco

Enter Marcellus

MARCELLUS

    The ship is ready to sail!

Exit Fortinbras, Horatio, Marcellus.

Scene 37: *North Sea, on a boat*

North Sea, on a boat.

Enter Fortinjambes, the Norwegian doctors and nurses and soldiers and sailing captain, Captain, Horatio, Marcellus, and Fortinbras

Fortinbras is at the whipstaff or tiller of the ship

Fortinjambes yawns.

CAPTAIN

    Your highness, you look halfway off to the land of dreams,

FORTINJAMBES

    I'm finally going home to Norway. I never expected my visit to Denmark would be extended for so long…

MARCELLUS

    Horatio, have you ever been to Norway before?

HORATIO

    I haven't. Apparently, its landscape is painted with fjords. I'm excited to see it.

MARCELLUS

    Me too.

FORTINBRAS

    Horatio, could you do please me a favour?

HORATIO

    What sort?

FORTINBRAS

    Tell the people down there, in the sea, that I can't ferry them.

HORATIO

    What? How?

FORTINBRAS

    It's easy. Just walk over to the edge of the boat, and shout into the sea that I don't know where the rivers Acheron or Styx are.

HORATIO

    That's ridiculous. I'd rather not play into this joke of yours.

FORTINBRAS

    Joke!? How dare you call it a joke! There's hundreds of people in the sea crying out for help, putting their hopes on me! You have to tell them to look elsewhere!

HORATIO

    I know nothing about these sea people you speak of! I can't hear anything you say they're saying, why are you asking me to do it?

FORTINBRAS

    Because among them, one says he's Hamlet, and another says she's Ophelia.

HORATIO

    How dare you!

FORTINBRAS

    Looks like somebody is angry Hamlet chose to speak to me over him!

SOLDIER

    Should one of the captains take over? I'm not sure if I want such an unreasonable man who has been almost sleepless for two days, as the commander of our ship.

FORTINBRAS

    Unreasonable? Talk to the captains, and they can note, that every command and turn of this ship has had no misstep! Sailing is my instinct. Horatio, I forgive you for your inactions. Let us move onto other discussion. What were you studying at Wittenberg?

HORATIO

    Medicine, among other things.

FORTINBRAS

    Ah ha! So you do have a fighting spirit against what has captured your parents, under the trapping shell of your situation's idleness!

HORATIO

    Then I must've lost it, because I haven't went back to Wittenberg, and I've forgotten my knowledge. The more I thought about studying there again, the more sadness weighed on my mind and stopped me to inaction.

FORTINBRAS

    You haven't stopped your dedication to Hamlet, even though his death and story brings you so much grief! Horatio, do your parents visit your dreams and scream that they're jealous of Hamlet?

HORATIO

    I don't know! How loud are the screams of all the men you've killed?!

SOLDIER

Someone, please! Stop this madness! It's infectious! The more I hear them speak, the madder I feel, and soon none of us will be able to realise we've arrived at Norway!

FORTINJAMBES

I have nothing for Horatio, but I have something that can silence Fortinbras.

DOCTOR 2

Fortinjambes stop, all will be for naught! Have mercy!

NURSE 1

You're already witnessing his fragility!

DOCTOR 1

You had sworn to secrecy!

FORTINJAMBES

Fortinbras, I can't bear to deceive you anymore. When we have arrived at Oslo, go straight to the castle, and talk to your mother. I want you to hear the details directly from your family. Because your mother loves you so much, she will be the first to break the silence. Ask for the location of your sister, and nothing except for that. People with fanciful stories will try to lead you astray. Insist on the location of your sister.

FORTINBRAS

Thank you for your honesty…

Captain, handle the ship for me.

CAPTAIN

> I will.

Fortinbras stares into the sea.

MARCELLUS

> Horatio, do you agree with me that there is clearly something wrong going on?

HORATIO

> The exact situation, we can only tell once we reach the castle, but I do believe there is something off.

Exit everyone

Scene 38: *Oslo Castle / Akershus Fortress*

Oslo Castle / Akershus Fortress

Enter Fortincoeur, Fortinbras, Horatio, Marcellus, Fortinjambes, Captain

FORTINBRAS

> Mother! I have nearly forgotten your face, it's been too long since I've seen you.

FORTINCOEUR

> Your face is rugged from where the sprays of the sea have often washed you. How is my new king of Denmark?

Enter Prince Norway

FORTINBRAS

    Terrible. Where is my sister?

FORTINCOEUR

    Isn't she right here, with you?

FORTINBRAS

    She is not. I repeat, where is my sister?

PRINCE NORWAY

    Fortinbras, I know your ears are not in need of repair. Please don't bother your mother like this.

FORTINBRAS

    Then I will bother you. Where is my sister?

PRINCE NORWAY

    We sent her away to be educated. Ladies like her need not to be taught to throw knives or personally perform… lengthy executions. She didn't want to upset you by leaving you alone in Denmark, or imply that you were a bad influence on her, so she forged an excuse for Amieoffille to take her place.

FAUXTINJAMBES/ AMIEOFFILLE

    From your mother only.

FORTINBRAS

    Please, mother. Tell me where she is. I will weep if you don't.

FORTINCOEUR

    It is better that you weep.

FORTINBRAS

    I will weep and root my body to this spot for eternity, until you tell me where she is.

Pause

FORTINCOEUR

    I've been told she has died. Slain, nearly a year ago.

PRINCE NORWAY

    Since the truth is uncovered, the rest might as well be unravelled. When Fortinjambes found out you become king of Denmark, that unruly woman hoped to voyage to Denmark herself, using one of your personal sailboats. Witnesses say someone who was a returned soldier from your army to Poland had fought her. They both fell and drowned, bleeding. There is nothing for you to do.

FORTINBRAS

    Of course she's dead, and some part of me sealed her fate! Dead, dead, dead, dead…

Fortinbras starts laughing uncontrollably

PRINCE NORWAY

    Guards! Take Fortinbras away to the cell.

Enter castle guards

MARCELLUS

    You can't kidnap him, he's the king of Denmark!

PRINCE NORWAY

    Does this laughing madman look like the king of Denmark to you?

HORATIO

    A part of him does.

PRINCE NORWAY

    Then I am sorry you had to deal with him.

Exit Fortinbras, castle guards.

HORATIO

    What lies in his future?

PRINCE NORWAY

    Nothing much. He will stay in the cell.

AMIEOFFILLE

    A cell!? How long will he be there for?

PRINCE NORWAY

    I will keep him in there until his humours have balanced, and he is no longer a liability.

And you, Amieoffille, you have failed what we asked of you in the most obscene way. He was supposed to be unaware of his sister's disappearance to avoid the madness that comes with stressing about it, yet he comes in here, asking for her location.

AMIEOFFILLE

>He deserved to know the truth instead of being constantly deceived.

PRINCE NORWAY

>And the truth has made him mad.

AMIEOFFILLE

>I was the one that witnessed him over the months, not you! The madness I saw was the build-up of several tragedies, the forged-letter being a spark to that fire. If I knew this would be the result, I never would have participated in it! He may have been prone to madness, but this deception's results have left him madder than any truth could. I couldn't bear to keep the deception running any longer.

PRINCE NORWAY

>Guards, this woman's business here is done. Please put her outside.

Exit Amieoffille, taken out by guards

Fortincoeur nearly exits, but decides to stay and listen.

PRINCE NORWAY

>I've recently heard about the disastrous state of Denmark, tales of Fortinbras being a beggar, and his general incompetence in times of disaster. I assume you people are here to ask for our help?

CAPTAIN

>Yes, we are.

PRINCE NORWAY

    Then the formalities can be skipped. Sweden had contacted us earlier, and I have prepared help for Denmark the moment I've heard of Fortinbras's failures to handle the situation. I will be on the fleet that will begin sailing tomorrow, and each ship has its own captain that will visit its allocated location in Denmark. Meanwhile, I will have the servants show you around the castle, the guest rooms, and I will hand the two Danes some money, so the city will be their delight.

CAPTAIN

    You are very kind.

Exit Prince Norway, Captain, Horatio, Marcellus, Fortincoeur

Scene 39: *Outside in Oslo, next to the sea*

Outside in Oslo, next to the sea

Enter Marcellus, enter Horatio

MARCELLUS

    Those mountains I see in the distance are beautiful. If only I had more time to see all of them.

HORATIO

    Yes, they're quite captivating. I'm surprised Fortinbras had a favourite horse prior coming to Denmark, there doesn't seem to be very much easy flat land for Mourner to run on.

Enter Amieoffille

AMIEOFFILLE

    Norway is home to some horses. They're short and round with light coloured fur though.

HORATIO

    If I recall your name correctly, being Amieoffille, your presence at Denmark and the forged letter spurred on Fortinbras's plans of going to sea and fighting the pirates.

MARCELLUS

    Let us be privy on this whole ordeal with Fortinjambes, you, and Fortinbras. After all, your actions had interfered with Dernmark's…

AMIEOFFILLE

    The fates of Fortinjambes and mine converged when she wandered onto a farm one day, and saw a girl that was her living reflection. We've been friends ever since. But soon after Fortinbras had become king, I was told she had been murdered. His uncle and cousin hired me to entertain Fortinbras with the illusion of his sister being alive. I would arrive in Denmark with these doctors and nurses, we'd keep watch on Fortinbras, wait for Prince Justin to clear the pirates, then venture back to Norway. After apparently seen his sister, he'd dismiss any incoming rumours as nonsense. He would never find out, and he would never go mad. At least, I was told that was the plan.

HORATIO

    But why forge a letter to do all this? Why did you introduce possibility of pirates in that meeting? The nation's budget being spent on the navy to fight them meant we couldn't withstand our crop loss.

FORTINJAMBES

If the pirates interrupted the connection between Denmark and Norway, he'd contact Norway less and avoid the passing rumours about his sister's death.

MARCELLUS

I do recall him using Swedish merchants to build the Navy instead of the usual Norwegians arriving on our shores.

HORATIO

So, does Norway know Fortinjambes is dead?

AMIEOFFILE

A few may know, but the witnesses had their silence bought. It's a miserable business being Fortinjambes. The pressure of a peasant woman being put in charge of Denmark! The unfortunate Danes having to live under my rule!

Fortinjambes doesn't even have a memorial, due to me taking her name. Nothing marks her absence, to slow the spread of this now-broken secret. Find the top of Norway, and place my eyes there. For her, my eyes can recreate all the fjords over this land!

Amieoffille screams at the sea.

AMIEOFFILLE

Finally, the sea can hold my pain… It's something we sometimes did. Horatio, Marcellus, if you have anything within you that you would like the sea to wash away, you can do the same.

MARCELLUS

The locals would think we are mad!

AMIEOFFILLE

Yes, you could be mad, let your anger out. I will tell any prying passer-bys that it's a Danish tradition!

MARCELLUS

I don't like the Swedes occupying our Elsinore castle! I've been there for a great part of my life, but now its inhabitants are replaced, including me!

Marcellus screams at the sea.

AMIEOFFILLE

Horatio?

HORATIO

I think I prefer to talk to the sea, to keep what is within close by me.

Horatio sits down.

HORATIO

(to himself and the sea) I'm afraid of madness, it has been all around me in my life. My parents, Hamlet, Ophelia, and now Fortinbras, madness or a resemblance to it, came for them one after the other. Fortinbras did tell me to say that he can't ferry the people in here. Now he has no more orders. I haven't liked him, but I've found myself directionless again. I don't know where to go.

Horatio stands up

AMIEOFFILLE

    Since Justin has given you two money, I will show you around town to see if there is anything that interests you.

MARCELLUS

    Thank you.

HORATIO

    Wait a moment.

Horatio screams at the sea.

HORATIO

    I thought it'd be fun.

Exit Amieoffille, Marcellus, Horatio

Scene 40: *Castle cells*

Castle cells

Enter cell guard

Enter Amieoffille, Marcellus, Horatio

MARCELLUS

    It's a grim way to end our tour of Oslo.

Enter Prince Norway

PRINCE NORWAY

May I ask, what are you three doing here?

AMIEOFFILLE

A servant told me this is where Denmark's king is. I'm leading these two Danes see their king one last time, before they go back to Denmark. It would be cruel if they didn't.

Horatio, Marcellus, I think he is here.

Marcellus is looking at an area somewhere.

MARCELLUS

That's horrendous... You've tied his entire body to a bed. How is he supposed to move, or do other bodily functions?

PRINCE NORWAY

It looks cruel, but it's a kindness. He cannot hurt anyone else and regret it, and he cannot hurt himself. If he needs to ask for something, he has his voice.

AMIEOFFILLE

Yes, but aren't you hurting him? Nobody, not even a snail, would enjoy becoming so immobile. And if he's so mad, then how would you know when to listen to him?

PRINCE NORWAY

His habits are known to us, since he has a history of them.

AMIEOFFILLE

The habits of why Fortinbras and Fortinjambes often turned to the sea has become known to me, if these hidden horrors could await them at home…

PRINCE NORWAY

Criticise all you want. There is no better way to deal with him than this.

HORATIO

It's strange to see a king like this, a mere man tied to a bed. The same body who was appointed to be in charge over lands further than his eyes can see, and legs can run. That one body can command hundreds or thousands of other bodies to build things and die for him. That in times of disaster, someone so small is supposed to lead everyone else to salvation.

All this power, all this burden, placed upon the fragility of one human.

PRINCE NORWAY

Yes, he is fragile.

HORATIO

You are too. You are a man as well, just like him.

PRINCE NORWAY

Such quick words. I will make the difference between him and me clear, and that is I have at least a modicum of responsibility and none of his madness or cruelty. When you are responsible and know how to command everyone to your advantage, your people's eyes are your own eyes, their hands are your hands. You are the mind, and your subjects are your body. If the ruler is fragile or cannot command his subjects, they won't lend themselves to him, leaving his body a mere single man.

What are your relations to him? Are you his friends?

MARCELLUS

    I'm a sentinel for the castle at Elsinore.

HORATIO

    I was his advisor, though he didn't ask me for advice very much.

PRINCE NORWAY

    Sounds exactly like what he would do. Consider yourself relieved of your non-duty. He will not bother you anymore.

Enter Fortincouer

PRINCE NORWAY

    Fortincoeur, he is asleep.

FORTINCOUER

    Has he been responsive ever since you've put him in there?

PRINCE NORWAY

    No. I talked to the guard earlier, and he said the only thing has happened is that he laughed, then cried, then stared at the wall, then fell asleep. Our words don't reach him, he acts as if he is deaf to us.

FORTINCOEUR

    Then I will try. Fortinbras!

Pause

FORTINCOEUR

    Fortinbras!

Pause

PRINCE NORWAY

    I'm afraid, this time the madness has taken him so strongly, that there is nothing left of him.

FORTINCOUER

    If he is just a body, then I would have buried him…

HORATIO

    I think he should be released. Having those ropes trapping his body to the bed might as well trap his madness to his body.

PRINCE NORWAY

    You sound like a man that has talked to Aksel.

HORATIO

    I have.

PRINCE NORWAY

    His fondness clouds his judgement to the reality. No dangerous persons will be released.

HORATIO

    Fortinbras wasn't dangerous. He was only laughing out of misery.

PRINCE NORWAY

    Which will always lead to a sudden desire for weapons. You have not dealt with him as long as I have. My decisions are sound.

Exit Fortincoeur

MARCELLUS

    If he is the king of Denmark, and there is nothing left of him, and Fortinjambes is dead, then who is ruling Denmark now?

PRINCE NORWAY

    Does he not have a steward!? Did he not appoint anyone to look after Denmark!?

HORATIO

    Two sentinels and his stable-hand rule Denmark now.

PRINCE NORWAY

    Two sentinels and his stable-hand cannot rule all of Denmark!

AMIEOFFILLE

    Says who? I was ruling Denmark for a small while, and I was a peasant posing as a princess.

PRINCE NORWAY

> This ridiculousness is why I, with great sorrow, will bear the weight of leading Denmark out of its disaster.

AMIEOFFILLE

> How convenient! Kidnapping Fortinbras so you can have both Denmark, and Norway once your uncle is gone!

PRINCE NORWAY

> You say as if this is a matter of my greed, but I assure you, the people of Denmark deserve a leader that is functional. I had held off interfering with Denmark's affairs until now, since I enjoyed having an entire sea separating my cousin and me.

AMIEOFFILLE

> If you're so functional, then why did you take so long to remove the pirates? You could have prevented Denmark's suffering!

PRINCE NORWAY

> The weather was not always favourable months earlier and would pose a risk to our people.

Amieoffille, you already have no further duty involved with the royal family, and you will not be allowed in the castle. I will have this guard escort you out.

AMIEOFFILLE

> Wait, what if I need to talk to Fortincoeur!?

Amieoffille is dragged out by the guard.

PRINCE NORWAY

It is a shame, but she is almost as unruly as the original. I do not need monitoring trouble-makers in the castle to be on my list of labours.

Tomorrow, I invite you two on my ship, back to Denmark. You should go to sleep early, we are sailing in the morning.

Exit everyone

Scene 41: *Ship on the North Sea*

Ship on the North Sea

Enter Horatio, Marcellus, other background people/ship-staff

MARCELLUS

It feels lonelier, with all the other ships in the fleet fanning out away from us, the sea becoming more and more our company in this journey.

HORATIO

There they go, delivering food and some builders to other parts of Denmark. I remember Prince Justin said this ship's destination, but I did not hear it well.

Enter Amieoffille

AMIEOFFIILE

We're going to a place called Skagen!

HORATIO

    Skagen…

AMIEOFFILLE

    I think someone said it was the most northern part of Denmark, so this ship will probably be the first to shore.

MARCELLUS

    Fortinjambes! How did you arrive here? I never saw you boarding the ship.

AMIEOFFILLE

    I climbed aboard using the strength of my legs and some other tools. I want to see Denmark again...

Enter Prince Norway

PRINCE NORWAY

    I see we have a stowaway.

AMIEOFFILLE

    If you want me to go, you're going to have to execute me!

PRINCE NORWAY

    Unlike Fortinbras who has no qualms about doing that sort of deed, I will do no such thing.

AMIEOFFILLE

    Oh, how I hate you!

You think so little of Fortinbras, fooled me into doing your ploy, and we have suffered immensely! I saw how devastated Fortincoeur was, and you had me dragged out before I could comfort her. You think removing me was the wise thing to do just because I was "unruly"?!

PRINCE NORWAY

      You're foolish if you think Fortincoeur would want to see someone with her dead daughter's face running around, constantly reminding her of what she had lost. You think I'm cruel, but I only had good intentions with the ploy, keeping Fortinbras sane. If I wanted to be greedy, I would have told him the news about his sister immediately, then ousted him while he was going through madness. But I didn't. Because I am kind.

AMIEOFFILLES

      Kind! You are saving Denmark from a problem that you helped cause. You torment your own family! Maybe I should torment you in return.

Amieoffille raises her fists in a fighting stance.

MARCELLUS

      (to Horatio) Do you think we should intervene?

HORATIO

      Amieoffille, if you would like to fight Prince Justin, please wait until we're on land. There's a chance both of you can be knocked overboard.

Amieoffille lowers her fists.

PRINCE NORWAY

      Thank you, Horatio… It is a shame Fortinbras didn't make more use of you.

HORATIO

I'm sensing clear distaste towards Fortinbras from you, and Fortinbras does not speak much about you. What rift is between you?

PRINCE NORWAY

It's only a natural rift between the intelligent, and simple minded, violent feral fools who need to be reined in due to having no control over their impulses.

AMIEOFFILE

What a shame there's no one to rein you in.

PRINCE NORWAY

And here you have a perfect exhibit of the latter type who is foolish enough to not notice that a certain member of our family needed my father to bribe him not to invade Denmark and cause a rift between our countries. That only he and his sister developed a "hobby" for personally executing the condemned as practice for killing King Hamlet.

AMIEOFFILLE

Calling me a fool!? When we reach land, I'll have a wager with you, Justin! We will fight with only our hands. If I knock you to the ground and win, I will be the queen of Denmark and you will release Fortinbras. If I lose, you will become Denmark's king.

PRINCE NORWAY

I don't participate in ridiculous wagers such as these. I decline, and I will become king of Denmark anyway.

AMIEOFFILLE

    Just you wait until you reach those shores…

HORATIO

    [aside] I should ease this frightening tension.

Your highness, had you known the former Prince of Denmark well?

PRINCE NORWAY

    I've heard of him, but I didn't know him well.

HORATIO

    I could tell you about him.

AMIEOFFILLE

    Oh, start from the start, when you first met him! Fortinbras told me about your unfinished letter to Fortinjambes and Fortincoeur, saying how wonderful Hamlet was!

HORATIO

    I will.

Scene 42: *Skagan Shores*

Skagan Shores

Enter Polish Tourist 1, Polish Tourist 2

POLISH TOURIST 1

    This has been the most unfortunate time to go visit Denmark for our travels! We should have stayed in Poland or ventured to some other country!

POLISH TOURIST 2

    But if we stayed in Poland, we wouldn't have found all this armour lying on the ground after the wind had come!

POLISH TOURIST 1

    Yes, I quite like it. They make us shine with a soldier's excellency! Oh look, a large ship has arrived on shore.

POLISH TOURIST 2

    I hope it's a cargo ship. I may look like a soldier now, but I'm not prepared to fight!

Enter Amieoffille, Prince Norway, Horatio, Marcellus, various background actors

Prince Norway is commanding the background actors to unload the cargo from the ship

POLISH TOURIST 1

    So it is. What do you think the cargo is for?

POLISH TOURIST 2

    Eating, I suppose. There's a lot of food, some construction materials, and people. Were these people planning to settle here?

POLISH TOURIST 1

    I don't know, but if the delivery is for us, they're extra blessings!

Amieoffille spots these Polish Tourists and runs up to them

AMIEOFFILLE

    Hello soldiers, are you from around here?

POLISH TOURIST 1

    I don't understand your language.

Amieoffille runs back to Horatio, Marcellus.

AMIEOFFILLE

    Can any of you talk to those soldiers? They speak a foreign language I don't recognise at all.

HORATIO

    So they must be not from Norway, Denmark or Sweden… I've been taught Latin. I will see if they speak it.

Horatio walks to the tourists.

HORATIO

    Hello, do you understand me?

POLISH TOURIST 1

    I recognise this as Latin! This one is probably a scholar. I don't know Latin though.

POLISH TOURIST 2

    I don't know Latin either. Let's stare at him until he goes away.

They stare at Horatio. Horatio walks away.

MARCELLUS

Did you discover their language?

HORATIO

I think they could be Polish. We had a few Polish students at Wittenberg, and they spoke similarly.

POLISH TOURIST 1

That one over there, commanding all the people delivering the cargo, I think he's their leader.

POLISH TOURIST 2

I wonder what he is here for. Let's talk to him.

The 2 tourists walk to Prince Norway.

POLISH TOURIST 1

Hello, leader of this arrival!

PRINCE NORWAY

I'm sorry, but I don't understand Polish.

POLISH TOURIST 1

He speaks the same language as that messy woman who ran to us.

POLISH TOURIST 2

They sound similar to the Danes. I think we should send a notice to our friend about this arrival, who can speak between us.

POLISH TOURIST 1

    Yes, I think we should. I will try to communicate to this leader about our intentions.

Polish Tourist 1 points to himself and Polish Tourist 2, does a jogging motion, points to his head, then points to his mouth and Prince Norway's mouth.

Exit Polish Tourist 1, Polish Tourist 2

PRINCE NORWAY

    Horatio, what is your interpretation of these odd motions?

HORATIO

    I think they will be retrieving someone that knows both the languages we speak.

AMIEOFFILLE

    Ha ha!

PRINCE NORWAY

    How does this situation bring you so much glee that you laugh?

AMIEOFFILLE

    Neither of us can have Denmark, if Horatio is right about these soldiers being from Poland. The Polish have taken over!

MARCELLUS

    Though I can still see the damages from the storms, the townspeople of Skagen seem to be active. I wonder if their activeness is due to Poland helping them repair the city.

HORATIO

The soldiers, I question their presence...

PRINCE NORWAY

If this place is already occupied, then I suppose we can keep some of the food for ourselves until we understand more of the situation, and send our help to the townspeople if they still need it...

Prince Norway motions for the ship's crew to carry the cargo and follow him.

Exit Prince Norway, ship's crew.

AMIEOFFILLE

Horatio, your stories about Hamlet were wonderful. I love how you bring Hamlet, all his intricacies, and the people around him, to momentary life with such detail in your recollections.

MARCELLUS

Before today, I have never heard of the stories about you and Hamlet at Wittenberg. It's wonderful to hear that Hamlet studied both books and people, and turned days you dreaded, into days you dreamt of.

HORATIO

Yes, meeting him was wonderful...

AMIEOFFILLE

    The young lady you've mentioned in your stories, this intriguing Ophelia, I often heard those in Elsinore's castle talking about her… Going mad and drowning herself, still so young. I had always envied noblewomen, but learning of her confusion and suffering, I wouldn't be surprised if I did the same had I lived her life.

Hmmm…Horatio? Did I say something wrong?

HORATIO

    No, it's not to do with what you've said.

MARCELLUS

    Then what is it? It has disturbed you suddenly.

HORATIO

    I'd rather not discuss it.

AMIEOFFILLE

    Is that so? Then while we're here, let's look at Skagen!

Exit Marcellus, Horatio, Amieoffille

Scene 43: *Skagen*

Skagen

Enter townspeople, Marcellus, Horatio, Amieoffille

Some townspeople are trying to repair their houses, along with Polish people, and people that came on Prince

Norway's ship. Amieoffille tries to help, but the strange-looking messy woman is shooed away.

They watch the townspeople doing repairs on their houses. Other people in Skagen are doing their own thing. Skagen's people aren't always in harmony, sometimes arguing.

MARCELLUS

    I don't mean this in a rude way, but both of you appear to have lost all desire in the idea of seeing Skagen.

HORATIO

    I never had any in the first place. I don't like the people in Skagen.

MARCELLUS

    What's wrong with the people of Skagen? They're Danes, just like us.

HORATIO

    Look at them all. They're miserable. Hungry. Fighting each other. In chaos. They're all disturbed… Disturbed, disturbed, disturbed…

AMIEOFFILLE

    Some families appear to be missing members who could have died at sea fighting pirates.

I can try blaming Prince Justin until my death, but seeing these Danes, I don't know what apology could suffice for taking part in shattering their families.

That ploy couldn't have functioned without me. If my guilt from taking part crumbles me, so be it. I will lie down here and have the ants consume all my flesh…

Amieoffille lies down and acts dead.

HORATIO

    No! How dare you!

AMIEOFFILLE

    You barely know me. Does it matter if I die or not?

HORATIO

    It doesn't matter whether I know you or not. I'm tired of seeing everybody die around me!

I am the most useless man in existence! I don't know why Hamlet ever picked this vagrant, and funded my desire for education, when my knowledge for medicine has become nothing and can help nobody! My parents were correct, my life never should have been. I repaid Hamlet's kindness by killing him, and everyone he loved!

MARCELLUS

    Horatio!? What do you mean by being the one that killed Hamlet?!

HORATIO

    If I didn't tell him about King Hamlet's ghost, he wouldn't have put on his antic disposition, worrying everyone else in the castle and leading to the series of disasters at Elsinore!

MARCELLUS

    If you didn't tell him about the ghost, he would have sooner or later found out, either by himself, or from one of us sentinels, then have done something about it. The disasters started with Claudius killing King Hamlet. Nothing you did has wronged young Hamlet.

HORATIO

    I have wronged him! Hamlet could always transform sorrow into laughter, and show me the beauty and wonder of life. But when he lost his father and his entire being seeped with sorrow, I couldn't do the same. I couldn't even help Ophelia from her madness nor keep good watch of her whereabouts… The last times of Hamlet's life, he was so alone, with his entire family and long-time friends, thinking of him as a madman. Even now, I have failed to help him. There are many stories passing through the country that murkify his true existence…

How can I claim to love Hamlet, but have wasted his attention and efforts in the way I have!?

MARCELLUS

    Hamlet's death was an event that I wish was avoided, but you were exactly what he wanted. He did not want a doctor, or to be joyful among the disaster at Elsinore, but he did want a trusted friend. He was entirely right to trust you, and you have always endeavoured to tell his story faithfully. While it is upsetting to live in a world that doesn't always value truth, whether others want to or don't, is not your failure.

HORATIO

Thank you Marcellus, I am always glad for your presence and words.

But still, my stark uselessness burns me…

Here, another person in front of me, no, my entire hometown crumbles, and I have no remedy.

AMIEOFFILLE

Is it so bad to be useless? Even if you are useless, I think you should live. Sometimes I catch some octopi while fishing, and they're rather useless to me, but I don't want them to disappear.

Amieoffille stops lying on the ground

AMIEOFFILLE

And you have helped people before. If it does any good for you, I'll get up off the floor right now. Then you won't think yourself useless, for you have helped another person.

MARCELLUS

Horatio, Amieoffille, let's continue wandering around Skagen, and see if anyone needs help with repairing their house. We won't solve all their problems, but we can help with simple things.

HORATIO

Yes, I suppose we can.

Exit Marcellus, Amieoffille, Horatio, and everyone else.

Scene 44: *Skagen Shores*

Skagen Shores

Enter Prince Norway, Horatio, Marcellus, Amieoffille, Polish Tourist 3

POLISH TOURIST 3

    A few days ago, I've received orders to look for you since you've landed a ship here. We want to know what it's about.

PRINCE NORWAY

    Who are you exactly? Are you the leader of the Polish around here?

POLISH TOURIST 3

    [aside] I suppose I am, since I paid for our trip to Denmark!

Yes, I am their leader.

PRINCE NORWAY

    I am Prince Justin of Norway. I had heard about Denmark's devastation, and had sent Norway's aid to various locations.

POLISH TOURIST 3

    We thank you very much, it has been a great help for us. We, the people of Poland, are very pleased by Norway's generosity.

HORATIO

    Are the Danish civilians alright!?

POLISH TOURIST 3

    Yes, of course. We are a peaceful arrival. If you have no more to say, then I will go.

PRINCE NORWAY

    Thank you.

Exit Polish Tourist 3

PRINCE NORWAY

    I will be returning to Norway. Since Poland now occupies parts of Denmark, and your king is absent, what plans do you two Danes have for your futures?

MARCELLUS

    I think I will stay in Skagen. If I hear that Elsinore is safe to travel to, then I will take the soonest ship there.

HORATIO

    Your highness, if it is alright for you, I will follow you back to Norway.

Marcellus, I suppose I must say good-bye to you for now. I hope living in Denmark won't be difficult, with multiple factions scavenging for our land.

MARCELLUS

    I hope so too. Good-bye Horatio, may Norway treat you well!

Marcellus hugs Horatio

AMIEOFFILLE

I'm going to Norway too! I have some business I need to do there… Good-bye Marcellus!

Marcellus waves

Exit Marcellus

PRINCE NORWAY

I have no obligation to harbour a woman who wanted to fight me on my ship.

HORATIO

I request that you allow her to come with us. I would like to speak with Fortincoeur. I believe Fortincoeur will be more open to speaking with me when I am accompanied by somebody she is familiar with.

PRINCE NORWAY

Amieoffille, you are only coming to Norway on my grace and favour for Horatio.

AMIEOFFILLE

Thank you, Horatio. I will help you find Fortincoeur. I was hoping to see her too.

Exit everyone

Scene 45: *Outside the Oslo castle*

Outside the Oslo castle, at Fortinjambes's grave

Enter Fortincouer

Enter Amieofffille, Horatio

AMIEOFFILLE

    I've found Fortincoeur…Fortinjambes… her grave is marked now!

FORTINCOEUR

    Yes…She has been waiting for you.

Pause

AMIEOFFILLE

    Fortincouer, does my phantom-like face bother you? Seeing me so lively, while your dear daughter is so lifeless. If it does, I will go.

FORTINCOEUR

    It is your face, as much as it is hers. I am glad that my daughter shares her image with someone as equally wonderful.

AMIEOFFILLE

    Her grave…It is beautiful, it is horrible…

She lowers herself and weeps at the grave…

Horatio tries to politely exit.

FORTINCOEUR

    You, young man. I have seen you before.

HORATIO

    Yes. I was at the castle earlier with your son.

FORTINCOEUR

You sound Danish… What has returned you to Norway?

HORATIO

I wanted to talk to you, but I've changed my mind. I have decided it is better not to pry into your personal matters.

FORTINCOEUR

Then I will pry into yours first, so you will feel no guilt. What has motivated you to come to me?

HORATIO

I suppose, to merely talk.

FORTINCOEUR

About what?

HORATIO

My own life has been speared down by various losses. Yours too, first your husband, then your daughter, and now your son's mind has lost its shape. I wonder why we live and keep going to the future.

FORTINCOEUR

At first I lived for the day King Hamlet would die a brutal death. But too many other things have happened. Now at least for me, I know my eventual death is a certainty, so I will wager on life's possibilities, no matter how meagre.

HORATIO

> Thank you.

Pause

HORATIO

> Is that Fortinbras looking at us, from that window up there?

FORTINCOEUR

> Yes, I had him released. While he can walk, he is unresponsive…

AMIEOFFILLE

> Oh no… He cannot even hate me for deceiving him for over half a year when I knew the truth the whole time. I betrayed him and partook in creating this consequence…

FORTINCOEUR

> I talked to him earlier about how this entire ploy had come to be. He remained in his silence since the moment I released him, but I sensed no anger towards you.

AMIEOFFILLE

> You are true to what you have said, he is unresponsive…

If I have no way to apologise to Denmark, then at the very least, I should apologise to him…

HORATIO

> I will follow. I also have something to tell him.

Exit everyone

Scene 46: *Inside the Oslo Castle*

Inside the Oslo Castle

Enter Fortinbras (holding a sword), a guard

Enter Horatio, Amieoffille

HORATIO

    Hello Fortinbras, we saw you staring at us through the window.

Pause

GUARD

    Your efforts are futile. His body is vacant of a mind.

AMIEOFFILLE

    Fortinbras? I know what I will say now is a late rope to a man, and many other Danes, who have drowned in consequences, but I've come here to apologise for my wrongdoing against you and to all of Denmark that has suffered from the consequences of my actions, my inactions, and my cowardice. I should have told you the truth the moment I saw you.

If you want to execute this peasant woman who has overstepped her role by horrific bounds, I will accept your vengeance for your own and Denmark's honour.

Pause

HORATIO

If there is anything left of you at all, I beseech, don't waste away and die! Are the consequences still in your mind!?

FORTINBRAS

So…you've returned…

Enter Prince Norway.

PRINCE NORWAY

You have been released and found yourself a sword!? And this woman is in here?

Fortinbras glares at Prince Norway.

Guard walks between Fortinbras and Prince Norway.

FORTINBRAS

Stay out of my business.

Exit Prince Norway.

FORTINBRAS

Horatio, it is true… I don't think I could truly leave, my soul's entrapment in Denmark has kept me here. There is something I would like to try. I will talk to you about this later…

Amieoffille, do you recognise the boat that held my sister's last moments?

AMIEOFFILLE

I've been told which one it was. The boat still sits peacefully on the water, as if it never held death…

FORTINBRAS

    Show it to me… When the sun has set, return to the water's edge where the boat is, along with my mother.

Horatio, if you would like to, you can come to the gathering…

Guard, you are not invited. Leave me be.

AMIEOFFILLE

    Follow me…

Exit Amieoffille, Horatio, Fortinbras

Exit guard

Scene 47: *Water's edge in Oslo*

Night, water's edge in Oslo, with the sailboat

Enter Fortinbras, Fortincoeur, Horatio, Amieoffille (nervously)

Fortinbras motions them to all stand at certain spot together.

Fortinbras raises its sails, untethers the boat, lights the boat on fire, and kicks it away.

The small gathering watch, as the flaming boat sails away into the night.

FORTINBRAS

    Farewell, dear sister…It had been awfully fun.

The last time I saw your face, you must have been that horrible omen in the sea. So frightened, frightening, and at unease…But thank you, for coming to visit.

AMIEOFFILLE

Perhaps doing the impersonation was causing these, but while I was in Denmark, I often saw visions of Fortinjambes. Many times when I was questioning or forgetting myself, I would see her dancing in the distant fields, just like she said she would when Denmark was finally hers. Reminding me of her existence…

FORTINCOEUR

Whether she is in hell, heaven, or in other places beyond humanity's reach, I hope she remembers and knows our love for her…

FORTINBRAS

Did you two actually see her die?

AMIEOFFILLE

No. Justin told me about it when he called me in.

FORTINCOEUR

I was told her body fell in the water so there was no body to look at.

AMIEOFFILLE

Do you think it's possible Justin killed her?

FORTINBRAS

I'd rather not start that sort of trouble without proof. Either way, I can't kill him, because I would have to rule

Norway in his place, and I can't subject more people to that.

Well... Whether she had died or if she hated all of us enough to run away and send no notice, this is farewell to her...

AMIEOFFILE

    Your majesty, for my treacherousness against your kingdom and impersonating your sister, if you would like to execute me for my crimes, then I'll face it.

FORTINBRAS

    Giving you my anger or losing you will accomplish nothing for me. Everything has been done, and nothing more will happen. Myself, I am not innocent in doing horrendous acts against others. I'd rather not continue doing it.

So go. Live your life. I know at least Fortinjambes would have been amused that you could do this sort of trickery for so long. She would be honoured by your strength and skill.

AMIEOFFILLE

    Really? No punishment at all after what I've done? That's incredibly... unfair. It's stupid!

FORTINBRAS

    I've never been renowned for my intelligence anyway, so do what you will.

AMIEOFFILLE

    I am still troubled by Denmark's losses though, so I will devise some way to bring that country joy, after I've brought it so much sorrow. I do not know how, but maybe some method will come to my mind eventually.

FORTINBRAS

    I wish you success in your endeavour.

Mother, I am sorry for worrying you for all this time, and now worrying you further. There is some business in Denmark I must attend to quickly, one of which is seeing my stable-hand. I will be leaving again, as soon as I can.

FORTINCOEUR

    So soon? If you must go, then you must go. It will be bearable. If Amieoffille has no objections, I would like her to stay with me for a while.

FORTINBRAS

    Horatio, you will come with me, and be returned to Denmark.

 I would like to talk privately with Horatio. He has been dealing with issues that he would rather not reveal.

For now, mother and Amieoffille, farewell, and good-luck with fighting Justin!

AMIEOFFILLE

    Poor Horatio! I hope things will be better for you soon. Good-bye you two!

FORTINCOEUR

    Take care, and don't do anything foolish!

HORATIO

We will try not to! Good-bye!

Exit Amieoffille, Fortincoeur

HORATIO

What issues have befallen me?

FORTINBRAS

If I said the issues were mine, they would never leave. By the way, I apologise for my ridiculous behaviour back when we were on the ship.

HORATIO

Thanks you.

FORTINBRAS

Now that we are alone, can you tell me what goes on in Denmark? Would it interfere with reaching that bush near Mourner's grave?

HORATIO

Last time I was in Denmark, Poland had taken the northern parts, though a soldier told me that the Danish civilians remained unharmed. The city I went to, Skagen, was recovering steadily. I don't know if Sweden still occupies Elsinore, but if civilians are left alone, then we should be able to visit Mourner's grave easily.

What are you planning?

FORTINBRAS

    Since that rabbit originated from and disappeared into that bush, I'm thinking of bringing a priest to exorcise that bush, and then I will kill both the rabbit and the bush with a blessed tool. What do you think?

HORATIO

    I've never dealt with possibly demonic rabbits originating from bushes before, so I have no other better idea.

FORTINBRAS

    Since the people of Elsinore still probably want my head, we will find a priest here to take to Denmark. I know the Captain has resided in this town, I will ask him to assist with the sailing.

Let's go.

Exit Fortinbras, Horatio

Scene 48: *A Church*

A Church

Enter Fortinbras, Horatio, a priest

PRIEST

    Your highness, have you come for another exorcism? Are you here to repent?

FORTINBRAS

    The exorcism is not for my own body this time. There is a place in Denmark where I had found a demon. If not dealt with, Denmark's havoc will continue.

HORATIO

    We would like you to follow us or find us a priest that is willing to come to Denmark.

PRIEST

    Those Danes have certainly been unfortunate. I will come.

Exit Fortinbras, Horatio, Priest

Scene 49: *Captain's house, outside*

Captain's house, outside

Enter Fortinbras, Horatio, Priest

FORTINBRAS

    I pray that he still occupies the same house.

Fortinbras knocks on the door

Enter Captain

CAPTAIN

    Fortinbras? You're well again? And I can see Horatio, and a priest too. What brings you all here?

FORTINBRAS

    My madness has subsided for now. As soon as you can, if you assist us in sailing to Denmark, then back to Norway after a stay shorter than a day in Denmark, you can have three of my sailboats, of your own choosing. Ask no questions about the reason for the journey's existence.

CAPTAIN

    Bribing me, eh? I will consider it.

Pause

CAPTAIN

    I will do it.

I will meet you all at the port in the morning.

Exit Fortinbras, Horatio, Priest, Captain

Scene 50: *North sea, on a boat*

North Sea, on a boat

Enter Fortinbras, Captain, Priest, Horatio

Fortinbras is at the whipstaff or tiller

Horatio is inspecting a long gun.

HORATIO

    You said I should have the gun to shoot at any rogues we meet at sea, but I'm not sure if I could.

FORTINBRAS

    Then sell it once we've reached Denmark. A hunter might like it.

Pause.

HORATIO

    Fortinbras? You're not that stupid. You can do many things I can't. Your abilities to navigate are astonishing. I certainly can't sail across these seas as well as you do, nor perfectly plan our arrival to Stockholm.

FORTINBRAS

    Thank you! I've practised a lot over my life. It actually makes me quite happy to hear that…

CAPTAIN

    Fortinbras, you have been sailing long enough. You should go to sleep. I will take my shift now.

Fortinbras sits down. Captain becomes the helmsman.

FORTINBRAS

    You have been as sleepless as me.

HORATIO

    At first, I suspected that sailing was enough to make any man sleepless, but the priest has rested.

FORTINBRAS

    Priest, how do you sleep so well?

PRIEST

    I lie down and close my eyes, the same way any other person does.

FORTINBRAS

    You do not fear the cruel realm of sleep that delivers visions of men's bodies being carved, rivers of blood, and sounds of soul-shattering screams?

CAPTAIN

    It is the same with you? I am less alone in one aspect of my life.

HORATIO

    Sleep brings me the corpses of Hamlet, my parents, and Danes that died in the storms…

Pause

FORTINBRAS

    Priest, why don't the exorcisms do away with this warlike-sleep and madness? If your exorcisms don't work, how will we know that you shall be able to drive out this demon in Denmark?

PRIEST

    My efforts may not be perfect, but it is better I try than not.

FORTINBRAS

    Do you ever wonder if your exorcisms didn't work because there was nothing demonic to be rid of? That God himself decided to send these torturous visions?

CAPTAIN

You can't say something like that. Why would God torture Horatio?

HORATIO

For my failures and weakness. I was too slow to follow Ophelia and stop her from drowning. I let Hamlet venture to that doomed fencing match against my concerns. I did not try hard enough to convince Fortinbras our existing navy was enough.

FORTINBRAS

Apart from you being slow at running, a task you said during the investigation of Elsinore's tragedy, was assigned to you and not something you volunteered your abilities for, you shouldn't believe you are weak because your words failed to pierce the brick wall of my skull. Or Hamlet's, who seems to have built his own wall before he died, based on what I've heard.

HORATIO

Thank you. I realise, I haven't been kind to you at all.

FORTINBRAS

Kind? For what? I certainly haven't earnt it.

HORATIO

Even before the disasters, ever since your arrival to Denmark, I've been impolite to you.

FORTINBRAS

    It's no matter now. I never expected you would have any politeness for the man who was planning to invade Denmark anyway.

HORATIO

    And I fear your words are also a blunted spear in my own brick wall. It's hard not to feel like it's punishment of some sort when your own mind torments you.

FORTINBRAS

    I understand God wanting to break my mind for my sins, and so I will take that punishment. But if torment breaks your clever and innocent mind, whether it happened by Godly intervention or the lack of it, whatever is left of me will bite my thumb at Him in the depths of hell!

PRIEST

    Please don't be so blasphemous while we're at the mercy of the sea!

A breaching humpback whale appears

HORATIO

    Did you see that massive fish?!

FORTINBRAS

    Yes, it crossed my sight!

CAPTAIN

    Where is it!?

PRIEST

      It was behind you, but now it is gone. It better not return to eat us.

Pause

The whale spouts some water in the distance

HORATIO

      There it is again!

FORTINBRAS

      Look at it, spitting water from the top of its head. Disrespectful!

CAPTAIN

      Where!?

PRIEST

      It escaped your eyes again…

HORATIO

      It was beautiful, but I'm relieved it's going away. Such a massive creature really could eat us all. Have you seen those whales before?

CAPTAIN

      Never. If it weren't for the fact that I clearly heard the fish this time, I'd have assumed that both you and the Priest have joined in on Fortinbras's continuing joke on me!

FORTINBRAS

    I've seen them a few times. I'm glad one hasn't swallowed me and put me in Jonah's position. God would never release me...

PRIEST

    You underestimate God's mercifulness. Your survival after witnessing these creatures several times is evidence of that. He only sent a disrespectful fish after your insult to Him.

HORATIO

    Is it really a bad omen? I thought at least some part of your life must have be blessed, to have seen Earth's wonderful creatures this many times. This is the first time I've seen one of those fish. I never knew something so large would try to fly out of the water.

FORTINBRAS

    It was the first time I've seen one of those fish spit so much out of the top of its head. I'm not sure if the liquid the whale expelled is actually spit at all. What kind of fish would need to expel so much spit into the air when they are already filled with water?

HORATIO

    Maybe the expelled fluid could from another bodily function, such as urine?

FORTINBRAS

    It's the only explanation I can think of. It travels to the surface, expels dirtied liquid for humanity to sail over and marvel at, then sinks back to the depths where it is clean!

CAPTAIN

Would God make such a foul creature that urinates from the head, and rises just to dirty our surface domain!?

FORTINBRAS

God designed every creature on earth! Priest, you're a man of God. Could you answer what exactly the whale is doing when it expels all that liquid?

PRIEST

Fortinbras, you have more pressing concerns in front of God than what kind of liquid a large fish expels from its head and its reasons for doing it…

HORATIO

Then ask God on behalf of me!

PRIEST

[aside] Why must I be trapped on a boat filled with gleeful madmen…It must be one of God's trials…

If you cannot pray for yourselves, then I will pray for you.

FORTINBRAS

Thank you…

Now all we have to do is wait for God's answer!

It is lucky we haven't met any pirates yet. Captain, when we reach Elsinore's shore, we will only be there for a short while. If there is anything you must do, such as stocking supplies for the return-trip, please do it as soon as you can.

Exit everyone

Scene 51: *Outside Elsinore Castle*

Outside Elsinore castle

Enter Swedish Ambassador, Swedish Soldier 1, other background soldiers

SWEDISH AMBASSADOR

    I can already see the Polish soldiers about to breach our borders. We don't have enough resources to defend these new acquisitions, especially when the storm had struck Sweden's south.

Pause

SWEDISH SOLDIER 1

    What brilliant luck! Is that Fortinbras approaching here, from that boat which recently arrived? What if we hand over this land to him, then he can do the dishonour of surrendering to Poland?

SWEDISH AMBASSADOR

    I don't know what he is doing here, but let's not waste Fortune's favour!

Swedish Ambassador gets a paper, places it on soldier's shield, quickly writes something.

Enter Fortinbras (holding a sword), Horatio (with a gun), Priest

SWEDISH AMBASSADOR

    Fortinbras, you look like a dead man walking! How about I revive your spirits, by having you return to being king of some part of Denmark? Sweden has decided to be generous, by returning any land Sweden has acquired west of the Sound Strait, directly to you! Here, take my pen and sign this treaty.

Fortinbras takes the paper and pen. Horatio is looking at somewhere offstage.

HORATIO

    Look at all those Polish soldiers over there, going in our direction.

FORTINBRAS

    I think I will wait a bit more, to fully form my decision.

Enter Polish Prince, Polish Soldiers.

POLISH PRINCE

    Swedish soldiers and Fortinbras? What is going on here?

FORTINBRAS

    It appears Sweden wants to surrender some of their Danish land to someone. Here, you can read the treaty.

Fortinbras hands the paper the Polish Prince.

POLISH PRINCE

    Are you going to take the land or not?

FORTINBRAS

    If I take it, then you would force me to immediately surrender anyway. How about we rewrite the terms, so that the surrendering of land is directly from Sweden to Poland?

SWEDISH AMBASSADOR

    As the Swedish ambassador and writer of the treaty, I say no to this amendment of the terms. If you want the land to go to Poland, then you must sign our treaty meant for you, then write your own terms of surrender to Poland.

Fortinbras takes the paper and signs it.

FORTINBRAS

    Horatio, I just remembered you never finished that letter to my uncle. For disappointing my uncle, I burden you with being the ambassador of Denmark. You can use your writing skills to write the terms of surrender to Poland.

Fortinbras gives the paper and pen to Horatio

HORATIO

    Somebody give me a shield so I may write…

Polish Prince beckons a soldier to let Horatio write on his shield.

Horatio writes the treaty on the back of the previous paper.

Fortinbras reads the treaty, writes an additional section, then hands it to Polish Prince.

Polish Prince reads it.

POLISH PRINCE

    We shall have all Danish lands west of the Sound Strait, and I will become king of Denmark. Beautiful.

Polish Prince signs the paper.

SWEDISH AMBASSADOR

    Something extremely peculiar must be going on. First, we never did find this pet rabbit which caused Fortinbras to almost immediately surrender this land because he wanted the rabbit to be spared during our takeover. Then, Fortinbras's arriving boat crew only consisted of four people, one of which has left on his own business. We have two men, a priest, and now both men have weapons. Is some sort of foolish duel to the death, with unmatched weapons, about to take place?

HORATIO

    Fortinbras is trimming a hedge with his sword, and I will shoot any birds hidden in there so we can eat them.

SWEDISH AMBASSADOR

    That doesn't explain the priest for the dead man's body!

Exit Fortinbras, Horatio, Priest, as quick as they can

POLISH PRINCE

    I hardly believe these men have come all the way here to surrender land and hunt birds for supper, running away from us with such urgency! I'm going to follow them to see this strange duel. Soldiers, you may follow me.

Exit Polish Prince and soldiers.

SWEDISH SOLDIER

    Perhaps they're duelling with unmatched weapons because Horatio convinced Fortinbras to surrender, and Fortinbras is mad over his lost honour and swordsmanship being doubted. I think he's trying to prove that he is skilled enough with a sword, to defeat even a gun!

SWEDISH AMBASSADOR

    It will probably be a bloody end, but I won't refuse the entertainment!

Exit Swedish Ambassador and soldiers.

Scene 52: *Grave with the bush*

Mourner's Grave with the bush

Enter Stable-Hand (with a horse prop), Fortinbras running in

STABLE-HAND

    What extreme luck! I wasn't expecting to see you while exercising one of the horses! You don't look well…

FORTINBRAS

    Don't worry about it. Sailing for several days can exhaust a man's beauty.

STABLE-HAND

    Are you certain about that?

FORTINBRAS

There is no doubt. Justin had delivered help to Denmark, so I am entirely glad.

STABLE-HAND

If you say so, then I'll trust you.

Enter Horatio and Priest

FORTINBRAS

Did anything from Norway come to Elsinore?

STABLE-HAND

Yes. They had arrived some days earlier, and had left a day ago. The people were happy to receive the supplies. So, you've returned to see Mourner's grave?

FORTINBRAS

Yes, and you too. I can tell you did the carved illustration of Mourner for the memorial, and it's beautiful. I'm only visiting here for a short-while, then I have to deliver the priest and Captain back to Norway, and I will probably stay there. How has life been in Elsinore?

STABLE-HAND

Despite the difficulties, I love it in Elsinore. The lands for the horses are much easier here, it's warmer, and the townspeople like me! Living here, I have the most friends I've ever had in my life.

FORTINBRAS

That's wonderful. Truly.

STABLE-HAND

    I wish you would stay here too. Maybe you could come back here, after you've returned the Norwegians.

FORTINBRAS

    It pains me to know that I will have to say farewell to you, because I'm not willing to stay in Elsinore. This place only holds bad memories for me now. But I am happy you have found a new home.

STABLE-HAND

    I think you might finally have to break your promise to me, about you employing me forever.

FORTINBRAS

    I'm sorry.

STABLE-HAND

    Don't be. I'm happy here in Denmark. And I'll come to see you in Norway when I can. Or you can come visit me.

Enter Polish Prince and all his soldiers, Swedish Ambassador and all the soldiers

STABLE-HAND

    How fantastic! All these people have come here to see Mourner's grave!

SWEDISH AMBASSADOR

    No, we didn't come here for a horse's funeral! If it's a funeral for a horse, then why would this Horatio person be given a gun? We're here for a duel, sword against gun!

STABLE-HAND

Why are you and Horatio duelling in this strange manner?

FORTINBRAS

We're not duelling…

HORATIO

(to Fortinbras) Since you already revealed part of the secret to the priest, I'm thinking that you should lift this veil of secrecy in the same way to our newfound audience, and take advantage of all these people that can help with the slaying.

FORTINBRAS

We're here to vanquish a demon that has been plaguing Denmark. First the priest will bless all our weapons. Then he will exorcise the demon out of the bush. Last time I saw it, it took the form of a rabbit. We will slay this demon, and destroy the bush that manifests it.

POLISH PRINCE

Should this demon be an existing thing, Fortinbras, for protecting our land from future devastation, I will forgive you for that battle over Polish land.

The priest goes on to bless everybody's weapons. Then he goes to the bush, and performs the exorcism.

Enter Rabbit (running out of the bush at extreme speed)

It manages to evade everyone's weapons, and exits the stage.

SWEDISH SOLDIER

    Why are you all in the army when you cannot hit even one rabbit!?

Horatio takes aim with his gun, and fires pointing offstage.

A thud is heard.

Everyone starts to cheer, in celebration for Horatio's success. Some people thrash the bush in celebration.

Someone tries handing Horatio the body of the rabbit, but he politely refuses.

POLISH PRINCE

    So it was true. Thank you, Horatio and Prince Fortinbras.

Exit Polish Prince and soldiers

SWEDISH SOLDIER 1

    Do you think we should eat the rabbit? Its demonic powers must be gone by now.

SWEDISH AMBASSADOR

    You can eat it by yourself.

[aside] That foul Fortinbras and Horatio, handing us demonic land so easily!

Exit Swedish Ambassador, Swedish soldiers, one of them is dragging the rabbit out.

STABLE-HAND

    That was somewhat eventful! Say, who is that man next to you? He seems familiar, but I can't seem to put a name to the face.

FORTINBRAS

    Do you speak of the priest, or the man with Adonis's likeness?

HORATIO

    If I become a proper doctor, my first act will be curing your blind eyes and truthless tongue!

STABLE-HAND

    A healer? By his words and appearance, I think that is Apollo beside you!

HORATIO

    My name is Horatio! Perhaps I should take you two's eyes for myself, to see how you both perceive such grandeur out of my ordinariness!

PRIEST

    Please don't try stealing eyes, that would be sinful.

FORTINBRAS

    Don't worry priest, we can trade our eyes instead. That way Horatio won't have six eyes, and us with none to perceive him!

STABLE-HAND

    Jesting aside, you do seem different, Horatio! There really is something more lovely about you! You look much like your usual self, yet somehow different enough that your presence lifts the air.

HORATIO

    Is that so? Thank you. Maybe it's from the relief that the demon shall no longer trouble Denmark.

FORTINBRAS

    What if the rabbit was innocent and I had imagined its demonic powers?

PRIEST

    It was exorcised, it must have been a demon.

FORTINBRAS

    Coincidence.

HORATIO

    Let us not worry about potentially demonic rabbits any further. That Swede was happy to have a meal, so let's leave the situation at that.

STABLE-HAND

    Ah, the horse is restless now. I must get going. Good-bye Horatio, good-bye Fortinbras, and come visit soon!

FORTINBRAS

    Farewell, Aksel.

Horatio waves goodbye.

Exit Stable-Hand and horse prop

FORTINBRAS

    [aside] So he is currently heading away from Elsinore…

    Horatio, the demon is slain. Denmark is safe, and your promised watch over me has ended. You are free to go.

HORATIO

    Actually, I'm thinking of riding the sailboat that delivered me here, back to Norway. I haven't seen enough of Norway, and I would like to see more of it.

But first, I want to visit Elsinore. I will tell them about the vanquished demon and see how the people are doing.

FORTINBRAS

    For your own sake, I prefer you go the other way. I've decided to go into Elsinore myself.

HORATIO

    Before the news about the vanquished demon is delivered? What task is so important in Elsinore, that you would risk walking into a town filled with people that still despise you and think you're demonic?

FORTINBRAS

    Consequences, Horatio. I will face my own consequences, and not just in thought.

Exit Fortinbras

HORATIO

    Didn't he plan to deliver you and the Captain back to Norway? This sudden impulse worries me.

Exit Horatio, Priest

Scene 53: *Elsinore town*

Elsinore town

Enter Townspeople, Fortinbras, Priest, Horatio

FORTINBRAS

    You two have followed me?

HORATIO

    I chose to go here.

They stand in the town. Townspeople walk by.

HORATIO

    They don't recognise you at all!

FORTINBRAS

    What a shame.

People of Elsinore! Here in front of you, is your former King Fortinbras! Anyone who wants to exact your vengeance may use this sword I've brought, or your own tools, against me!

People start staring, whispering, or gathering their own tools.

PRIEST

    I will intervene! Do not exact vengeance against him. If you are concerned about possible demonic influence, I've recently exorcised a demon found near Elsinore, and the demon was slain. There is nothing demonic in him.

If you have personal matters against him, do not dirty yourselves with murder. He has gone through madness, and as you can see, he has weakened considerably and become ineffectual. God's judgement has been, is, and will be upon him.

Fortinbras mouths some bad words.

PRIEST

    Think of as many foul words as you want, but I have done what I should, for your sake, and the sake of the people in Elsinore.

Exit Fortinbras, losing himself in a crowd of people, so the priest cannot follow.

Enter Marcellus, Bernardo, Francisco.

FRANCISCO

    I heard a strange scene going on in the distance…

BERNARDO

    If it weren't for that fact that I know everyone in town, I wouldn't have believed that was Fortinbras himself, instead of a local madman…

MARCELLUS

    Unfortunately, I could recognise him. He still doesn't seem well at all.

Look who's here! It's Horatio!

HORATIO

    Marcellus! You've made it back to Elsinore!

MARCELLUS

    I miss living in the castle, but living here is fine too.

FRANCISCO

    Horatio, have you decided to join us in living in Elsinore under Polish occupation?

HORATIO

    I haven't decided where I will be settled for now. I came here to see how Denmark is doing, and extremely soon, I will be travelling back to Norway to look at the landscape more. Last time I was there, I didn't look at the landscape as extensively as I wanted to.

MARCELLUS

    Have fun in Norway, Horatio! Should you ever decide to come live in or visit Elsinore, we will welcome you warmly.

HORATIO

    Thank you. And I will be glad to see you.

Enter a child with a stick that whacks Horatio, enter another older child following that one.

HORATIO

>Child, what are you doing!?

YOUNG CHILD

>I'm Mad Hamlet the Slayer, and now you're dead!

OLDER CHILD

>I'm also Hamlet, and as someone that recognises that man as the Horatio who has visited our town before, I say that he is not dead!

YOUNG CHILD

>I will kill someone else then! No one can escape my stick of justice!

Exit the children

HORATIO

>What is going on? Why have they become Hamlets?

MARCELLUS

>Some of the Swedish people that occupied the castle found your writings documenting the Elsinore Tragedy. They thought that the events were so intriguing, that they decided to turn your account of the Elsinore Tragedy into a play. It's become quite popular.

HORATIO

>It is rather strange to know that there are now players portraying me, and even stranger that such a recent tragedy has become amusement. I can't say that I like it, but if Hamlet's tale will go on, so be it…

MARCELLUS

I almost forgot to ask, how are the princes of Norway and Amieoffille?

BERNARDO

Amieoffille? Who's that?

MARCELLUS

It's a strange story. I shall tell you later.

HORATIO

Prince Justin is fine. Amieoffille, I believe she is staying with Fortinbras's mother. She might come back to Denmark. As for Fortinbras, I am worried about him…I can't tell if he was deceiving me on his wellness for quite some time, or he had a sudden lapse, but that scene in town seemed to be an impulsive decision.

MARCELLUS

I think that man in the distance is him, heading towards the graveyard.

PRIEST

I will follow him.

Exit Priest

Enter Captain

HORATIO

Captain! I wanted to tell you that I will be back on that boat returning to Norway.

CAPTAIN

>You are? Then I will get additional supplies.

HORATIO

>Thank you, captain.

Good-bye former sentinels!

MARCELLUS, FRANCISCO, BERNARDO

>Good-bye Horatio!

Exit Horatio

Exit Marcellus, Francisco, Bernardo

Exit Captain, and everyone else

Scene 54: *Graveyard*

Graveyard with refurbished Hamlet's grave

Enter Gravedigger, Fortinbras

GRAVEDIGGER

>Fortinbras, you've been standing there for a while. You know, the era of your rule had given me the most employment. I would have had a lot more, if all those men weren't swallowed by the sea where I can't bury them!

Pause

Ah, so there is life in you after all! Eyeing Hamlet's grave. The look on your face is almost telling me that I should dig a grave for you! If you want one so much, give me some payment. Though I can't guarantee it will be as beautiful as Hamlet's, or my cousin's dark ocean grave…

Pause

Enter Priest

FORTINBRAS

      Go away!

PRIEST

      After all these years, you still want to behave as moodily as you did when you were a child?

FORTINBRAS

      Yes I do! Leave me alone!

Priest steps away.

Enter Horatio

HORATIO

      I'm here…

It is sad to see many memorials have been broken.

Though Hamlet's grave…

GRAVEDIGGER

      Something broke his grave too, but the Swedish people somehow loved Hamlet so much, his grave was reinstated. Looks like you will have a place to cry at after all! In fact, I think this is the first time I've seen you cry at Hamlet's grave during the daytime!

HORATIO

    Yes, now I have no shame in showing my grief for him. It will be with me forever, and I will carry it into my own grave.

This time, these tears are not just for grief though. There is joy. Joy in knowing that Hamlet's story is beloved. The world's love for you will last past my lifetime, and will live for ages.

FORTINBRAS

    It is nice to see that you are so happy…

HORATIO

    It is happiness I never knew I would recover.

Fortinbras, now that I think of it, why exactly did you make me your advisor, if you rarely asked for my advice for most of your rule?

FORTINBRAS

    While you were recounting the events as the witness of the Elsinore tragedy, I saw the gloomiest man in the world, and thought he should at least feel important.

But I knew I could at least take advice from your face. If you were ever found smiling for a whole day, then I would know I had done well as a king…

It seems you have found your happiness anyway.

I've stood here long enough. I'm going back to the boat.

HORATIO

    I will follow you.

Exit Fortinbras, Horatio, Gravedigger, Priest

Scene 55: *Water's Edge at Oslo*

Water's Edge at Oslo

Enter Fortinbras, Horatio

FORTINBRAS

    The priest and captain has already been returned to their daily lives. Why must you follow me? I told you that you were free to go. You don't have to be my advisor anymore. You don't have to keep watching me. Don't you have the rest of Norway to see?

HORATIO

    I know there's something wrong here. You didn't recover any of your personal possessions from Aksel, then you did that scene in Elsinore, then you suddenly decided to give the Captain all your sailboats. Looking at you, you almost shamble around. The blaze is gone, there are only the last embers left, before all is ash.

FORTINBRAS

    I've only recently recovered from a bout of madness, you can't expect me to look so well. There's nothing wrong with sudden inspiration to be extremely generous to my friend, and a man who helped saved Denmark's future. If you're lacking something to do, why don't you go find Amieoffille and tell her that she could serve the Danes by overthrowing the Polish? Just leave me be.

Exit Fortinbras, Horatio

Scene 56: *Lonely water's edge, somewhere in Norway*

Lonely water's edge, somewhere in Norway

Enter Fortinbras

FORTINBRAS

    I never expected that a slow scholar would chase me all the way here…

Enter Horatio

HORATIO

    Where are you going, so far away from people?!

FORTINBRAS

    Horatio, I command you, as a Prince of Norway, that you leave. Sometimes people would like their privacy, and sometimes I enjoy wandering alone, free to go wherever, directed only by my own thoughts…

HORATIO

    You won't get any privacy. Not when you're behaving rather erratically, and I'm extremely concerned about what will be.

Fortinbras pulls out his sword, and points it at Horatio.

FORTINBRAS

    Leave…

Horatio checks if his gun is empty, then holds his gun like a sword.

HORATIO

    It would be an easy fight since I have no fencing experience, but if you want me to leave, you will have to fight me for it!

Fortinbras turns his sword over. He gives Horatio his own sword.

FORTINBRAS

    Another gift from me to you, to remember me by. Now leave.

HORATIO

    I'm not leaving.

FORTINBRAS

    If you're so insistent on staying, then use these weapons to mix my blood into the water. Take my place as prince. Your clever mind will serve you well.

Horatio throws both weapons into the water/offstage.

HORATIO

    You know I would never do that!

FORTINBRAS

    Horatio, can you hear it?

HORATIO

    Hear what?

FORTINBRAS

    Shhh!

Pause

The sea is singing to me. An entire choir! There's my father, my sister, and my daughter. They think I'm an incompetent disgrace.

There's all the men I've killed too. They have one wish. They will grab my body and sink me into the ocean so that I can never shed blood again.

The demonic rabbit is slain, Denmark has survived. All that is left is to dispose of this body and awake in Hell.

Farewell, Horatio.

There is a happy life ahead of you.

HORATIO

    I won't be happy to watch you die. You've stood against madness for so long, I don't want to see you sink yourself now! Is it every mad person's fate, condemned to make their own deaths?!

FORTINBRAS

    Perhaps. It doesn't matter. You don't need to watch this body leave. You will miss nothing important if you go now.

If, for some unknown reason, you want Fortinbras, look for him in the sea. I saw his sister in there too, once.

Fortinbras tries to exit/go into the water. Horatio drags him back.

HORATIO

What about your mother? Or Aksel, or Amieoffile, or your ever-prying uncle? Won't they miss you?

FORTINBRAS

Haven't I brought them all enough trouble already?

Norway's future is safe in Prince Justin's hands. You've probably heard all about Fortinbras from Prince Justin, and he will have said no false words. No country needs a violent incompetent.

The world can function perfectly in my absence. Please, let me go.

Fortinbras tries to exit. Horatio drags him back.

FORTINBRAS

Let me go! Has reason vanished from your brain?! Every message from God is wishing for me to suffer for my crimes. I am responsible for the deaths of hundreds, if not thousands, of people. If there was ever a criminal I should execute, it would be me! I should go as soon as possible, so the people of earth will no longer be subject to my destruction!

HORATIO

My reasoning has been temporarily banished, emotions currently rule! Do you think I would stand by and watch another prince die in front of me, have another person drown himself, when this time I am not helpless against the outcome? Have your death along with Hamlet's, Ophelia's, and my parents', haunt me for the rest of my days, and possibly drive me to madness? I will make Hell know your absence! Please, stay on land. I will forever blame myself for failing to have stopped you. I will cry over your dead body!

FORTINBRAS

Horatio, you are a cruel man. You know what to it is like to be unafraid of death, to desire its embrace. The only peace, the only rest, I can possibly have, is to cease what is left of this existence, yet you want to continue the torture that is my life. You, of all people, who would know how torturous it is to live past what is necessary.

HORATIO

Yes, but I've changed. I've lived long enough to realise the beauty of life all around me again. In the lands, the seas, the people, even God's ridiculous creatures, such as that giant disrespectful fish!

So I won't have your death undo my happiness! I don't want to grieve over you.

FORTINBRAS

You've become strong enough to survive after Hamlet. We're not even friends. You can survive my absence.

HORATIO

But I don't want to. I chose to be here! You may have incredibly frustrated me, and done many horrible things, but you and your schemes are part of why I have lived long enough to realise that I do want to live. If you wonder why you have someone that is so insistent that you live, you only have yourself to blame! I am merely repaying my debt to you!

FORTINBRAS

    Horatio. I will give you the last favour of removing your debt. Release your arms from me.

If you don't, our drowned doom is shared. Your grim fate won't be on anyone's conscience. This dead body will have none.

Fortinbras manages to finally exit stage/go into the water, dragging Horatio, who is still struggling to pull Fortinbras back, with him.

Silence.

Splashing sound offstage.

Fortinbras drags Horatio back on stage.

FORTINBRAS

    Fortinbras is gone, and all that is left is a coward. Horatio?! Horatio!? Is there any life left in you!?

How could you be such a knave? You had finally found your own happiness in life. Yet you were so willing to discard all your efforts in a blink, for somebody whose existence should be washed away…

How horrible am I, to have attempted to destroy your miracle.

HORATIO

    I breathe… I am breathing!

FORTINBRAS

    Horatio… You survived my murder!

HORATIO

    Yes! And you survived your own murder too!

Fortinbras, I want to be your friend.

I see you now. Not as someone who fails to be Hamlet, not as a prince tied to the goal of trying to avenge his father, not as a king who must prove himself or save his own people, but as a fellow man.

FORTINBRAS

    I'm not sure if I am capable of becoming a man like everybody else, or what I will be doing… I've lived my entire life as royalty. I cannot escape my own consequences from being one, if I were to meet someone who disliked what I've done. Or what if my madness returns and prevents me from thinking? Then what?

HORATIO

    I don't know.

FORTINBRAS

    Even you admit you might be lost when those situations come.

HORATIO

    But please, at least promise me, your mother, yourself, or anyone, your presence tomorrow.

FORTINBRAS

    Why?

HORATIO

      I asked your mother how she handled her losses. She told me that she had not left the mortal realm because death is an eternal certainty, so she takes on life's chances. The possibilities may be bad or good, utterly predictable, unexpected, or extremely painful for that day, but whatever will happen, I believe new lives awaits us, and I want you to be there trying to live yours. So, please, just at least for tomorrow, will you be there?

Pause

FORTINBRAS

      Then I…

I will take the wager.

I will see you tomorrow.

Horatio and Fortinbras exit stage together.

End notes

You've reached the end of the story.

Years after I've written the story, I'm not sure how I feel about it, my feelings are mixed. I'd like to think of it as a thing that existed in its moment in time back when it was written.

About the author:

I won't reuse an alias connected to this story for future stories.

I do not have social media connected to this story.

Any contact details you find related to this story could be or is outdated.

Beware of impersonations.

As of 5th of July 2025, my author page is at:

https://books2read.com/ap/n9BLL9/

or at https://horatioandfortinbras.wordpress.com/

though this information is not guaranteed to remain true forever.

Thank you. And good-bye.

Addendum:

Recently, I found out the person who had taught me *Hamlet* in school had passed away some years ago.

People can have any opinion on my writing ability, but I know that from having been in her class, she was a great teacher whom I am glad to have met. Thank you, Margaret.